Federico García Lorca

## Literature and Life Series
(Formerly Modern Literature
  and World Dramatists)

Selected list of titles:

Complete list of titles in the series available from publisher on request.

# FEDERICO GARCÍA LORCA

*Felicia Hardison Londré*

FREDERICK UNGAR PUBLISHING CO.
NEW YORK

Copyright © 1984 by Frederick Ungar Publishing Co., Inc.
*Printed in the United States of America*


**Library of Congress Cataloging in Publication Data**

Londré, Felicia Hardison, 1941–
  Federico García Lorca.

  (Literature and life series)
  Bibliography: p.
  Includes index.
  1. García Lorca, Federico, 1898–1939—Criticism and interpretation. I. Title. II. Series.
PQ6613.A763Z73736   1984     868'.6209     82-40270
ISBN 0-8044-2540-X

# Contents

# Chronology

1898    June 5. Federico García Lorca is born in Fuente Vaqueros in the province of Granada, Spain. He is the first child of Federico García Rodríguez and Vicenta Lorca Romero.*

1909    The García Lorca family moves to Granada.

1915    Lorca enrolls at the University of Granada.

1916    June 8–June 16. Lorca makes the first of four trips in central Spain with his class in Theory and Literature of the Arts. The other class trips are in October 1916, May 1917, and late summer 1917.

1918    April. *Impressions and Landscapes* (*Impresiones y paisajes*) is published in Granada.

1919    Lorca goes to study in Madrid, where he lives at the *Residencia de Estudiantes* until 1928.

1920    March 22. *The Butterfly's Evil Spell* (*El Maleficio de la mariposa*) is produced in Madrid.

1922    June 7. Lorca reads poems from *Deep Song* (*Poema del cante jondo*) at the Alhambra Palace Hotel in Granada. June 13–14. The Festival of Cante Jondo organized by Lorca and Manuel de Falla is held in the Alhambra in Granada.

*In Spanish-speaking countries, one's surname is formed by combining the patronymics of both father and mother, putting the mother's paternal name last; García Lorca is the correct form of Lorca's surname, but his own tendency to refer to himself by his mother's name alone has become standard practice among critics.

1923  January 5 or 6. Lorca and Falla present a Festival for
      Children to celebrate Twelfth Night.
      February. Lorca receives his law degree from the Uni-
      versity of Granada.
1925  Spring. He spends Holy Week with Salvador Dalí's
      family at their homes in Cadaqués and Figueras.
1927  May 17. *Songs* (*Canciones*, written 1921–1924) is
      published.
      June 24. *Mariana Pineda* is produced in Barcelona.
      The production opens in Madrid on October 12.
      June 25–July 2. Twenty-four drawings by Lorca are ex-
      hibited at the Dalmau Gallery in Barcelona.
1928  March 9. The first issue of *Cock* (*Gallo*) is published.
      April. The second and last issue of *Cock* is published.
      July. *Gypsy Ballad* (*Romancero gitano*, written 1924–
      1927) is published.
      Summer. A serious emotional crisis causes a prolonged
      psychological depression in Lorca and eventually mo-
      tivates his trip abroad.
      Salvador Dalí goes to Paris.
1929  January. Lorca finishes *The Love of Don Perlimplín
      with Belisa in the Garden* (*El Amor de Don Perlimplín
      con Belisa en el jardín*), but the play is censored and
      not produced until 1933.
      March. Lorca meets Chilean diplomat Carlos Morla
      Lynch.
      June 11–12. Lorca leaves Spain, traveling by train to
      Paris.
      June 16–18. He visits London and Oxford.
      June 19. He sails from Southampton on the S.S. *Olym-
      pic*, arriving in New York on June 25.
      July 2 or 3. Lorca moves into Furnald Hall at Colum-
      bia University.
      July 8–August 16. Lorca attends a summer session
      course in English for foreigners.
      August 18–28. Lorca visits his friend Philip Cummings
      at Lake Eden Mills, Vermont.
      August 29–September 18. Lorca visits Angel del Río
      in a vacation home near Shandaken, New York.
      September 18–21. He visits Federico de Onís in
      Newburgh, New York.

September 21. He moves into John Jay Hall at Columbia University.

October. Lorca withdraws from classes at Columbia University. He writes his film scenario *Trip to the Moon* (*Viaje a la luna*).

1930    Lorca moves into an apartment at 542 West 112th Street in New York.

March 5. Lorca leaves for Cuba, traveling by train and boat. He arrives in Havana on March 7 and lectures there on March 9, 16, 19, and April 6.

June 12. Lorca sails from Cuba on the *Manuel Arnús*, which sails for Spain on June 19, after docking for one day in New York.

August 22. He finishes writing *The Audience* (*El Público*, published in 1976).

December 24. *The Shoemaker's Prodigious Wife* (*La Zapatera prodigiosa*, written in 1926) opens in Madrid.

1931    April 12. General elections in Spain bring the end of monarchy and proclamation of the Second Republic.

May 23. *Deep Song* (*Poema del cante jondo*, written in 1921) is published.

August 19. He finishes writing *When Five Years Pass* (*Así que pasen cinco años*).

1932    July 10. The premiere performance by *La Barraca* is given in the public square of Burgo de Osma.

Late July–August. Lorca travels with *La Barraca* in Galicia, Asturias, and Santander.

1933    March 8. *Blood Wedding* (*Bodas de sangre*) opens in Madrid.

April 5. *The Love of Don Perlimplín with Belisa in the Garden*, written in 1928–1929, premieres in Madrid.

October 13, 1933–March 24, 1934. Lorca visits Buenos Aires, with a side trip to Montevideo, Uruguay, in February.

1934    March 27. Lorca sails for Spain on the *Conte Biancamano*, which docks in Río de Janeiro on March 30–31, and arrives in Barcelona on April 11.

August 11. Ignacio Sánchez Mejías is wounded in a bullfight and dies two days later. In September Lorca writes his *Lament for Ignacio Sánchez Mejías* (*Llanto por Ignacio Sánchez Mejías,* published in 1935).

December 29. *Yerma* opens in Madrid.

1935     May 11. *The Puppet Theatre of Don Christóbal* (*El Retablillo de Don Cristóbal,* written in 1931) opens in Madrid.

December 11. *Doña Rosita the Spinster* (*Doña Rosita la soltera*) opens in Barcelona.

1936     January. *First Songs* (*Primeras canciones,* written in 1922) is published.

June 19. He finishes *The House of Bernarda Alba* (*La Casa de Bernarda Alba*), which is produced posthumously in Buenos Aires on March 8, 1945.

July 16. He leaves Madrid for Granada to be with his family on his saint's name day.

July 18. St. Federico's Day. The Civil War begins.

August 9. Lorca goes into hiding at Luis Rosales's house in Granada.

August 16. Lorca is arrested and taken to the Civil Government in Granada, where he is detained until August 18.

August 19. Lorca is shot at dawn and buried in an unmarked grave in an olive grove near the village of Viznár.

# 1

~~~~~~~~~~~~~~~~~~~~~~~~~~~~~~~~~~~~

# The Artist's Life

Passion for life was the driving force behind Federico García Lorca's personality and his art. That passion for life imbued him with a deep-seated fear of death and made death a central theme in all his works. It nourished an intensity of mood ranging from the joyful exuberance of his frequent all-night poetry-music-wine-and-conversation sessions to the unfathomable depressions in which some of his most inscrutable poetry is rooted. His abundant vitality is reflected in the great number of close, lasting friendships he maintained, as well as in the multivalence of recurring symbols throughout his work. His desire to live fully and intensely led him to embrace all the arts: he was not only a poet and a playwright, but a platform speaker/personality, a composer, a pianist, a guitarist, a painter, a stage director, a set designer, a puppeteer, and a film scenarist. The development of that complex personality and his vast creative output during little more than two decades, prematurely cut short by his violent death in 1936, may be seen as a synthesis of innumerable impulses. His last years were devoted almost entirely to theatre as a form of poetry in which all the arts are integrated.

Lorca's lyrical and dramatic sensibilities were already developed during his early childhood in Andalusia, the ancient kingdom of southern Spain often associ-

ated with flamenco guitar, Moorish architecture, and an
abundance of fruits and flowers. He felt at one with nature on his father's fertile farmlands in the province of
Granada, where he conversed with ants and heard the
branches of the poplars sing his name. "My earliest
memories of childhood have a flavor of earth,"[1] he later
said, nostalgically summing up those years in simplest
terms: "shepherds, meadows, sky, solitude."[2] He as-
cribed his lyrical gift to that practice of seeing and hearing the simple authentic detail in everything.

The beginnings of Lorca's dramatic development
were vividly recalled by his family and their household
servants. Taking the role of the priest, he would reen-
act the entire Mass, familiar to him from regular atten-
dance at the village church with his mother; his impassioned sermons, however, were original and sometimes
brought tears to the eyes of the maids whose atten-
dance he solicited. Eventually, his dramatic representa-
tions at home became less dependent on ritual, and he
cajoled the maids into taking part with his brother
Francisco (Paco) and sisters Concepción (Concha) and
Isabel in performances based on the Andalusian folk-
lore, romances, and songs those peasant women taught
him. "What would become of little rich children," he
was to ask in 1935, "if it were not for their servants,
who put them in contact with the truth and emotion of
the people?"[3] When he was seven or eight, a troupe of
gypsies with a marionette theatre presented some puppet farces in the village, and this inspired the toy-
theatre productions for which he devised scenarios and
created elaborate sets and costumes.

Lorca always considered that he had enjoyed a
"very long, very tender, very joyous childhood that
never ceased to illuminate his life and art."[4] Indeed,
images of children and childhood occur throughout his
work. Asked what traits he had inherited from his parents, Lorca cited his father's "passion" and his mother's

"intelligence." Lorca's father, Don Federico García Rodríguez, listed his occupation on Lorca's birth certificate as "farmer and landowner."[5] He had first married Matilde Palacios Ríos, who died childless and left him a fortune. He then married Vicenta Lorca Romero, schoolmistress in the small town of Fuente Vaqueros where Lorca was born on June 5, 1898. Lorca's father was a stocky, dark-complexioned Andalusian who loved horses and music. An expansive and energetic man, he worked hard and was successful enough to add a number of estates to his holdings in the province of Granada. Doña Vicenta, a small-boned, cultivated woman and a skilled pianist, created a gentle, affectionate home life for her four children. Also living with the family until her marriage was Lorca's Aunt Isabel, his father's sister, who taught Lorca to play the guitar.

When Lorca was only two months old, his life was endangered by an undiagnosed fever that left him frail and retarded his development. Although he readily hummed the folk tunes he heard around the house, he was not able to talk until he was three, or walk until he was four years old. Favoring her oldest child because of his illness, Lorca's mother taught him the alphabet and to read music before he started attending school in the village. Doña Vicenta's former colleague, Don Antonio Rodríguez Espinosa, took a special interest in the sensitive child, and Lorca adored the kindly schoolmaster whose republican sympathies and musical inclinations were expressed in his pupils' singing of *La Marseillaise* at the end of each school day. When Don Antonio took a position at the Escolapian Fathers' Seminary in Almería, seventy-five miles away, Lorca's parents sent the devoted pupil to live in Don Antonio's house and to study at that school's institute. Those studies were interrupted by a mouth and throat infection; as Lorca later recounted it: "I was on the brink of death, but nevertheless asked for a mirror, in which I saw my swollen face; and since I could not speak, I wrote my first humorous poem, comparing myself to the fat sultan Marruecos Muley Hafid."[6]

In 1909 Lorca's family moved to Granada in order to provide more advanced education for their children. Although he missed the open atmosphere of the countryside, Lorca was enchanted with Granada because of its refined stamp of Arabic culture left from the Moorish occupation of four hundred years earlier: flowing water in innumerable public fountains, narrow streets creating shady respite from the glaring Andalusian sun, private patios heavily perfumed by lush vegetation, and, above all, the delicately filigreed arches of the fourteenth-century Alhambra Palace on a hill near the heart of the city. Granada is the subject of some of Lorca's most lyrical prose and poetry as well as the setting of one of his last and best plays, *Doña Rosita the Spinster*. Lorca believed strongly that the sensuous and mystical Arab ethos represented the finest flowering of Spanish culture, unfortunately repressed by the puritanical strictures of triumphant Catholicism. He summed up his feelings about Granada in a phrase borrowed from the Grenadine poet Soto de Rojas (1648): "paradise closed to many, garden open to few."[7]

In Granada, Lorca was sent to a private secondary school, the Colegio del Sagrado Corazón (Sacred Heart School), whose director was Doña Vicenta's first cousin. The most lasting effect of that phase of his education was to be his caricature of a pretentious aging professor of rhetoric in *Doña Rosita the Spinster*. More important to Lorca were his musical studies with Don Antonio Segura Mesa (1842–1916), who had been a disciple of Verdi. Don Antonio taught Lorca piano, harmony, and composition, and helped him analyze works ranging from the great classics of musical literature to traditional Spanish folk airs. Playing the piano became as natural to Lorca as conversation. He gained a local following for his ability, but could not persuade his father to let him study music in Paris after Don Antonio's death in May 1916.

An examination administered by the Granada General and Technical Institute was required for the baccalaureate, and this Lorca failed in October 1914. He spent the rest of that academic year taking courses at the institute and failing several more examinations, apparently because of his "nonconforming" penmanship.[8] He finally received the baccalaureate in May 1915 and enrolled in two degree programs at the University of Granada. To please his father he studied law, a traditional pursuit of upper-middle-class Spaniards. He followed his own inclinations in enrolling simultaneously in the Faculty of Philosophy and Letters. Most of his friends recalled that he read extensively, particularly Spanish poets like Cervantes, Lope de Vega, Calderón de la Barca, Tirso de Molina, and Góngora, as well as some foreign literature, certainly including Maurice Maeterlinck.[9] However, he did not apply himself to his formal studies and failed three courses. Several professors, recognizing Lorca's artistic gifts, were willing to overlook his scholarly lapses. Among these was Don Fernando de los Ríos, a law professor who was to become Minister of Public Education during the Spanish Republic and Ambassador to Washington during the Spanish Civil War; his only daughter married Lorca's younger brother Francisco.

One of Lorca's classmates, José Mora Guarnido, published a revealing anecdote from that period of Lorca's life: although Lorca's father was strict with his family about coming to dinner on time, Lorca never found it easy to regulate his activities by the clock and often arrived home after the family had sat down at the table. If Lorca joined them during the soup course, Doña Vicenta could usually pacify her husband, but one evening Lorca returned when the main course was well underway. Don Federico barked: "Do you think that our house is an inn? This had better be the last time you come late to dinner! Starting tomorrow if you're not here on time, you won't sit at the table!"

"Then I won't sit down!" Lorca replied. "I can't shut myself in the house just to eat when it's twilight!" The rest of the family was dumbstruck at Lorca's rebellious outburst and waited anxiously to see how the head of the household would handle it. Just then the cook entered and innocently asked what kind of omelette Lorca would like. His father responded furiously: "Give him an omelette of chrysanthemums! of violets! of twilight!" Peals of laughter broke the tension and both adversaries saved face. "Omelettes made of twilight" became a family joke that was invoked thereafter whenever Lorca was late.[10]

In 1915 Lorca joined the Granada Center for Art and Literature, where he gave a number of informal piano concerts. Two years later that club's journal published his first piece of literary criticism, "Fantasía simbólica" (Symbolical Fantasy), an article written for the centenary of the Romantic poet José Zorrilla. Since the center was considered the home of "establishment" art in Granada, a younger group of artists and intellectuals formed their own circle in which to discuss new trends in the arts. Lorca and Mora Guarnido frequently joined others of this group which took its name, *El Rinconcillo* (the little corner), from the fact that its members gathered informally in a corner of the Cafe Alameda on the Plaza del Campillo. Occasionally, Don Fernando de los Ríos dropped in, as did the great composer Manuel de Falla after he settled in Granada in 1919. Lorca and Falla quickly established a close and lasting friendship.

One university course was particularly important in Lorca's artistic development: Theory of Literature and the Arts, taught by Professor Martín Domínguez Berrueta. He organized as class projects a series of trips to various sites in Andalusia and Castile to explore the roots of Spanish literature. Careful research by Lorca scholar Ian Gibson has established the itinerary of the four trips that Lorca took with Berrueta and his classmates in 1916 and 1917.[11] On the first trip, from June 8 to June 16, 1916, in Baeza, Lorca met the great contemporary poet Antonio Machado. The little group of students was lionized in the small towns they visited, and their evening seminars, always culminating with Lorca at the piano, were glowingly reported in local newspapers.[12]

Lorca's notebooks from those class trips were the basis of his first book, a collection of prose sketches entitled *Impressions and Landscapes (Impresiones y paisajes)*. His friends of the *Rinconcillo* had always thought of Lorca as a musician; surprised at the literary merit of the essays he read to them after his travels, it was they who urged publication. Before assuming that expense, Lorca's father consulted Fernando de los Ríos and Manuel de Falla. He did not mind spending several thousand pesetas, but he was concerned lest his son become a laughingstock. Reassured that the work had literary merit, Don Federico financed publication by Traveset in Granada, and the book appeared in April 1918, with a cover designed by Lorca's friend, the painter Ismael de la Serna.

*Impressions and Landscapes* is dedicated to the memory of Don Antonio Segura Mesa, "whose hands so often went to the piano and wrote rhythms on the air . . . ." The book is the earliest concrete testimony to Lorca's multivalent artistry. In its numerous musical references and precise visual imagery, Lorca's lyrical prose reveals the sensibilities of a musician and painter as well as of a poet:

The sky began to compose its symphony in the minor key of twilight. The color orange was spreading its royal robes. Mel-

ancholy gushed from the distant groves of pine, as they
opened their hearts to the limitless music of the Angelus.[13]

There are, too, hints of the dramatist-to-be in the anecdotal passages with snatches of dialogue that deftly
sketch a character or capture the essence of a way of
life, and in the use of dramatic build and contrast as the
reader is led through the streets of a village or along
a series of interior passages. Although Lorca was later
embarrassed by the overblown style of that work, it
marked a turning point in his artistic development: music never lost its importance to him, but after 1918 he
knew that his vocation was literary. He later wrote in a
terse, third-person autobiographical sketch that since
his parents would not permit him to go to Paris to continue his musical studies, "García Lorca channeled his
(dramatic) impassioned creative drive into poetry."[14]
The parenthesis is significant.

In 1919 Lorca went to study in Madrid on the advice of Don Fernando de los Ríos, who recommended
Lorca's admission to the famous *Residencia de Estudiantes* (Students' Residence). Founded in 1910, the
*Residencia* was a center of intellectual life as well as a
residence for gifted students, whether they were enrolled at the University of Madrid or studying independently at the Prado Museum, the National Library, or
elsewhere. Set in a park on a hill overlooking Madrid,
*"la Resi,"* as it was familiarly called, comprised four residence halls, a library, a dining room, and a large central hall for meetings and lectures.[15]

Lorca lived at the *Residencia* for nine years, returning several times a year to Granada for long visits to
his family either in town or on one of their country estates. He spent many evenings at the piano in the *Residencia's* great hall, surrounded by friends who were
drawn by the infectious pleasure he took in singing and
playing the piano or guitar, and by his recitations of the

poems he wrote. The artistic stimulus of performing and conversing with friends was far more important to him than any formal studies, for he made no use of the law degree he completed in Granada in 1923. Among Lorca's contemporaries who lived in or visited the *Residencia* were future poets who would later be grouped with Lorca as members of the "Generation of 1927": Rafael Alberti, Manuel Altolaguirre, Emilio Prados, Pedro Salinas, and Jorge Guillén. The great poet Juan Ramón Jiménez, an earlier resident, frequently paid return visits, as did Antonio Machado upon occasion. Another resident was Luis Buñuel, later famous as a filmmaker.

Lorca's closest friend at the *Residencia* was Salvador Dalí, who came from Catalonia, the northeasternmost province of Spain, to study painting in Madrid. Already influenced by cubism, Dalí was far more avantgarde in outlook than his teachers at the School of Fine Arts, and his arrogance and eccentricity led to his suspension from the school in 1922 and his permanent expulsion in 1926. Dalí found more congenial company and intellectual stimulation at the *Residencia*, in a small circle that included Lorca, Pepin Bello, and Luis Buñuel. In the spring of 1925, Dalí invited Lorca to spend Holy Week at his family's seaside home in Cadaqués. Dalí's father and his sister Ana María were enchanted with Lorca, who subsequently visited on several other occasions and exchanged frequent, affectionate letters with Ana María Dalí. It was at the Dalí home that Lorca first read aloud the final version of his play, *Mariana Pineda*, which later had its premiere in Barcelona, the capital of Catalonia and the most receptive city in Spain to modern European literary and artistic currents. Lorca regarded the elder Dalí as a second father.

The intense, intimate relationship of Lorca and Salvador Dalí lasted until 1928 and was reflected in

their influence on each other's creative impulses. The
painter's poetic sensibilities were aroused, and the poet
admired the nonconformist painter's vision. They each
dabbled in the other's artistic medium, and they took
one another as subjects for their drawing and writing.
In his 1952 autobiography, Dalí wrote of Lorca (with an
oblique reference to their never fully explained break):

The personality of Federico García Lorca produced an immense impression upon me. The poetic phenomenon in its
entirety and "in the raw" presented itself before me suddenly
in flesh and bone, confused, blood-red, viscous and sublime,
quivering with a thousand fires of darkness and of subterra-
nean biology, like all matter endowed with the originality of
its own form. . . . And when I felt the incendiary and communicative fire of the poetry of the great Federico rise in wild,
dishevelled flames I tried to beat them down with the olive
branch of my premature anti-Faustian old age.[16]

One of Lorca's more interesting evocations of Dalí
is found in a 1927 letter to Sebastian Gasch:

Each day I become more sensitive to Dalí's talent. . . . What
is most moving to me about him at present is his *delirium* of
construction (that is to say, of creation), in which he aims to
create from *nothing* by dint of efforts made and thunderbolts
hurled with a faith and intensity that seem unbelievable.
There's nothing more dramatic than this objectivity and this
quest for joy for the sake of joy. . . . Dalí arouses in me the
same pure emotion (and may Our Lord God forgive me) as
does the infant Jesus without shelter in Bethlehem, with the
entire germ of the crucifixion already latent beneath the straw
of the manger.[17]

Among Dalí's recollections of Lorca at the *Residencia,* the following passage is noteworthy:

At least five times a day Lorca alluded to his own death. At
night he could not get to sleep unless several of us went to
"tuck him in." Once in bed, he still found ways to prolong in-
definitely the most transcendental poetic conversations of the

century. Almost always he came around to discussing death and especially his own death.

Lorca acted out and sang everything he spoke about, notably his demise. He staged it by miming it: "There," he used to say, "that's how I'll be at the moment of my death!" After that, he would dance a sort of horizontal ballet that represented the jerky movements of his body during the funeral, when the coffin would descend a certain steep slope in Granada. Then he would show us how his face would look several days after his death. And his features, which were normally not handsome, would suddenly acquire a halo of unaccustomed beauty and even excessive prettiness. Then, at the effect he had just produced in us, he would smile, elated with the triumph of having taken absolute lyrical possession of his audience.[18]

Lorca's 28-strophe "Ode to Salvador Dalí," published in the *Revista de occidente* in April 1926, is further testimony to the artistic and personal attraction that existed between the two. The antepenultimate verse of that ode is apparently a declaration of the poet's and the painter's mutual artistic reinforcement:

> But above all I sing a common mode of thought
> uniting us in dark and golden hours.
> Art is not the light that blinds our eyes.
> It's first of all love, be it friendship or fencing match.

> *Pero ante todo canto un común pensamiento*
> *que nos une en las horas oscuras y doradas.*
> *No es el Arte la luz que nos ciega los ojos.*
> *Es primero el amor, la amistad o la esgrima.*[19]

Marcelle Auclair succinctly evokes the importance of Lorca and Dalí to each other from 1922 to 1928: "One cannot speak exactly of an influence of one upon the other, but of a multiplication of one by the other."[20]

The first production of a play by Lorca occurred early in his Madrid years, even before he met Dalí. This came about after poet Eduardo Marquina intro-

duced Lorca to Gregorio Martínez Sierra, director of
Madrid's Eslava Theatre. Martínez Sierra was a prolific
poet-playwright who had won international renown
with his own dramatic masterpiece *Cradle Song (Canción de cuna,* 1911), and he, like Lorca, was fond of the
poetic dramas of the Belgian mystic Maurice Maeterlinck. When Martínez Sierra heard Lorca recite some of
his early nature poetry, including the anecdotal,
177-line "Encounters of an Adventurous Snail," Martínez Sierra saw dramatic possibilities and urged Lorca
to write a play about the lives of insects. Lorca wrote
an atmospheric allegory of love and death with poetic
dialogue, which he called *The Slightest of Plays (El
Menor de las comedias),* but Martínez Sierra retitled
it *The Butterfly's Evil Spell (El Maleficio de la mariposa)*—although Mora Guarnido has pointed out that
Lorca himself always avoided using words like "spell,"
"curse," or "sorcery."[21] Most of the characters are cockroaches, but all have human personalities: the bourgeois housewife, the coquette, the proud and wealthy
matron, the pious mouther of platitudes, the pragmatic
laborer. The dreamy boy cockroach, who writes love
poems and paints himself with pollen like a dandy, falls
hopelessly in love with a wounded butterfly whom the
cockroaches are nursing back to health and guarding
from the predatory, habitually drunk scorpion. Although the ending of the play has been lost, the boy
cockroach's death is clearly foretold.

Martínez Sierra did not stint in producing the play:
the company's leading actress, Catalina Bárcena, was
cast as the boy cockroach; the much-acclaimed dancer
La Argentinita (Encarnación López Júlvez) interpreted
the role of the butterfly; settings were designed by
Mignoni and costumes by the Uruguayan painter Rafael
Barradas. Lorca attended rehearsals and became convinced that the play would fail, but was talked out of
withdrawing it. The prologue, spoken by an actor in

evening dress, should have helped put the unusual work into perspective for the Madrid audience that was more inclined toward French farces in translation. (According to Lorca's friend, Melchor Fernández Almagro, the curtain raiser to Lorca's play was just such a piece of fluff, entitled *Columbine is Mad*.[22]) In the prologue, one may detect echoes of Lorca's childhood in the country: "Why should you be repelled by the clean and shiny insects that move so gracefully through the grass? And why are you, human beings with all your sins and incurable vices, disgusted by the good worms that travel serenely across the meadows taking the sun on a warm morning?"[23]

The first—and only—performance of *The Butterfly's Evil Spell*, on March 22, 1920, was a complete disaster. Many in the audience laughed, hooted, and called out wisecracks in response to the insect talk. They were, in fact, reflecting the attitude of Doña Cockroach, whose narrow-minded intolerance of her son's poetic inclinations spoofs a bourgeois response to art. Lorca's friends in the audience rallied to his defense, but he tried to pacify them during intermission, saying: "I am 'visibly moved,' as they say in the newspapers, but I am 'invisibly' quite calm. To me this audience means nothing, nothing, nothing." In the reviews that appeared the following day, some critics admitted that they had not been able to hear much of the play. The overall tenor of the critics' responses accorded with that of *El Imparcial*: "A play about cockroaches—ugh!" At the same time it was generally agreed that the author had a talent for poetry.[24]

Lorca remained grateful to Don Gregorio for having taken a chance on a twenty-two-year-old, but the experience nonetheless held in check for seven years his inclination toward the theatre. He concentrated on writing poetry and satisfied his strong dramatic instinct by his frequent recitations among friends. Lorca was an archetypal exemplar of the strong musical and vocal tradition in Spanish poetry; performance was a necessary corollary to the text of his poems. His magnetic personality and his unforgettable voice—as well as the poems themselves, transmitted orally in widening circles by fellow students and their acquaintances—won Lorca a reputation as an important poet even before the publication of his first book of poems. José Luis Cano recalls "a liquid, dark and warm voice, sometimes roughened by gaiety or sorrow. And his voice often had the musical accompaniment of his equally unforgettable laughter, that tremendous deep-toned laughter . . . generously lavished with the natural energy of his radiant youth, his irresistible congeniality, his superhuman charm that won over all listeners."[25]

Lorca's orientation to poetry as a performing art explains his lifelong habit of carelessness with his manuscripts; he often gave away his poems without keeping a copy. As late as 1933 he told an interviewer that he took no pleasure in publication: "Everything I've published has been wrested from me by editors or friends. I like to recite my verses, to read my work aloud. But then I have a great fear of publication. This fear comes when I copy down my things and I already begin to find flaws, and frankly they no longer please me."[26] For that reason, there is often little relationship between the dates of composition and the publication dates of Lorca's poems. His first published volume of ,poetry, *Book of Poems* (*Libro de poemas,* 1921), dedicated to his brother, contains sixty-six poems, mostly written from 1918 to 1920, but even at the time of that publication he was already moving beyond those simple, lyrical nature poems that exhibited various literary influences to a more focused and individual style based on his love for Granada and its music.

*Deep Song (Poema del cante jondo),* written in 1921–1922 but not published until 1931, was directly inspired by Lorca's involvement, with composer Manuel de Falla, in organizing the Festival of Cante Jondo, which was held in the Alhambra in Granada on June 13–14, 1922. *Cante jondo,* or Andalusian deep song, combines intensely emotional yet stylistically spare poetry on themes of pain, suffering, love, and death with a primitive musical form that bears traces of Byzantine Catholic liturgical chant (used in Spain until the eleventh-century adoption of the Roman rite), songs of the Moors, who occupied Spain from 714 to 1492, and, most importantly, the ancient Oriental musical forms brought by the gypsies from India between 1400 and 1450; a possible Jewish influence in certain Sephardic rhythms has also been suggested.[27] The purest forms of *cante jondo* were the *siguiriya gitano* and the *soleá,* which Falla and Lorca believed were in danger of eclipse. The *saeta,* or unaccompanied Passion song, had retained its purity and was kept alive by its long association with the church's Holy Week. Such variations as *serranas, polos, cañas,* and unaccompanied *martinetes, carceleras,* and *livianas* also retained traditional qualities that set them apart from corrupt modern *flamenco* forms like the *malagueñas, grenadinas, rondeñas, sevillanas,* and *peteneras.*

With the stated goals of reviving, preserving, and purifying *cante jondo,* Falla and Lorca organized a competition open only to nonprofessional *cantaores* (singers) and their accompanying guitarists. Apart from the commercialized *flamenco* music, gypsy deep song had become associated in the middle-class Spanish mind with vice-ridden ports and dirty taverns in ethnic ghettos of Andalusian towns, despised much as was Negro blues singing in the United States at that time; but the reputation of the ascetic and devoutly Catholic Manuel de Falla gave the project a stamp of respectability. Finally, the Granada Center for Art agreed to sponsor the competition, and the city subsidized it with twelve thousand pesetas. Lorca helped to win the support of Granada's artists and intellectuals with his lecture on "Primitive Andalusian Song" at the Center in February. During the next few months he and several others traveled around Andalusia seeking out true *cantaores* in the small villages. Years later he recalled:

You arrive in a village where someone's said you'll find one of those prodigious men. You wander in the streets, and window curtains are lifted as you pass, then dropped. You prowl about the square giving small coins to children. Two old men are seated on a bench. You sit down on another bench. You watch the sun eat the shade, and perhaps you stay long enough to see the shade eat the sun in its turn, but something tells you not to budge. . . . Then, suddenly, from the throat of one of the old people comes a modulation, to which the other responds. . . . They sing in dialogue, very low, for themselves alone. . . . They sing *por seguiriyas* or *por soleares*. They have thin voices, but your blood freezes: the *jondo* bursts forth, completely vital, from those cracked voices. And their right feet, scarcely audibly tapping, mark time set apart from time, which is one of the mysteries of *cante grande*.[28]

Lorca returned from those travels with new poems inspired by the rhythms and themes of the *cante jondo*, including his famous "Guitar" (*La Guitarra*) and "Poem of the Saeta" (*Poema de la saeta*), which were later collected in *Deep Song*. On June 7, as a prelude to the festival, a gathering in the ballroom of the Alhambra Palace Hotel heard guitarists Andrés Segovia, Manuel Jofré, and Niño de Baza, followed by Lorca's recitation of some of those poems. *El Defensor de Granada* reported the next day that "the evening belonged to Federico García Lorca. . . . Granada has a poet. This boy, a dreamer who loves what is beautiful and sublime, will achieve greatness."[29]

The competition dates were chosen to coincide with the full moon. On the nights of June 13 and 14, four thousand people assembled in the Alhambra's

Plaza de los Aljibes, which was ornamented with lanterns and garlands of flowers. The women in the audience wore their family heirlooms: embroidered silk and
satin shawls, jeweled combs, fragile lace mantillas and
fans. The stage was decorated with Grenadine tiles and
rugs. On the jury with Falla were, among others, guitarist Andrés Segovia and the aging master *cántaor* Antonio Chacón. The latter was so stunned by the *serrana*
sung by seventy-three-year-old Diego Bermúdez, the
grand prize winner, that he crossed himself and ex-
claimed softly, "Dear God! what do I hear!" Bermúdez
had walked all the way from Puente Genil to Granada,
a distance of over a hundred kilometers. Another winner was a youth named Manuel Ortega, who later became the famous Manolo Caracól. The Festival of Cante
Jondo did achieve its purpose of arousing the public's
awareness of its Andalusian folk heritage, and in the
process strengthened the friendship of Lorca and Falla.

A second collaboration of Lorca and Falla took
place only six months later, when they organized a children's puppet show for Twelfth Night, the Feast of the
Three Kings. The audience that assembled in the
García Lorca house at 33 Acera del Casino in Granada
was composed of a hundred local children and about
twenty adults. Lorca designed the scenery and costumes, which he and two friends constructed. Falla arranged music by Debussy, Albéniz, Ravel, Pedrell, and
Stravinsky; he directed the musical ensemble, which
included a clarinet and a lute, and he played the piano.
Vocal solos were sung by Lorca's sister Isabel and her
friend Laura Giner de los Ríos. Lorca and his sister
Concha operated the puppets. The program was composed of three short plays: *The Two Chatterboxes* by
Miguel de Cervantes: *The Girl Who Waters the Basil
and the Inquisitive Prince (La Niña que riega la alba-
haca y el príncipe preguntón)* by Lorca, based on an
Andalusian folk tale; and the anonymous twelfth-cen-

tury *Mystery Play of the Three Kings*. Although the cloth backdrops painted by Lorca are still in existence, the text of his play has been lost. It initiated a series of puppet plays and popular farces that were to become an important facet of Lorca's work.

In Lorca's gradual synthesis of his interests in poetry, music, painting, and theatre, 1927 was a pivotal year. He not only achieved public recognition in each of those areas, but he also, finally, reconciled his father to the fact that he would never have a more "serious" vocation than that of an artist. The previous year, after giving an original and insightful lecture on the early-seventeenth-century poet Luís de Góngora, Lorca had written to his friend Jorge Guillén: "Sometimes it surprises me when I see that I am intelligent. Old age!"[30] A few months later, evidently reacting to his parents' concern that at twenty-eight he was not yet financially self-supporting, Lorca wrote to Guillén asking advice on how to become a professor of poetry. Lorca saw that course of action as a way of reconciling his parents' desire to have him settle into a profession and his own realization that he could "neither eat nor drink nor hear anything that wasn't Poetry."[31] The need to devote himself entirely to poetry soon suppressed the thought of finding regular employment.

In 1927, Lorca's second volume of poetry, *Songs (Canciones)*, was published. Written between 1921 and 1922, this varied collection of transitional poems is notable for its "musical sensuality." The poems for the most part combine the hard-edged imagery of the European avant-garde (ultraism) with "contrapuntal melodies wherein the opposition of a dual theme is constantly seeking resolution in a single harmony, somewhat in the manner of a fugue."[32] A month later, Margarita Xirgu's company presented Lorca's historical verse drama about Granada's nineteenth-century folk heroine, *Mariana Pineda*, with Margarita Xirgu in the

title role, at the Goya Theatre in Barcelona. Salvador
Dalí designed the scenery and costumes, and Lorca directed a children's chorus that sang the ballad at the beginning and ending of the play. Praised by critics for its
lyrical expression and its themes of love and liberty, the
play was moderately successful with the public.

On June 25, the day after the opening of *Mariana
Pineda*, an exhibit of twenty-four colored drawings by
Lorca opened for one week at the Dalmau Gallery in
Barcelona. Lorca's new friend, critic Sebastian Gasch,
reviewing the exhibit in the Catalonian-language journal *L'Amic de les Arts*, referred to the works as *"poesía
plástica,"* or "modeled poetry."[33] After that summer of
1927, Lorca had only nine years left to live. Those nine
years proved to be just sufficient to complete the process of forging the pure poetry of words, the visual poetry of the painted image, and the aural poetry of his
music into the all-encompassing poetry of the theatre.

In December of 1927 the Ateneo of Seville invited
a number of young poets to a literary conference at
which they would lecture and recite their poetry. This
week-long cultural event was organized by the highly
literate and cultivated *torero* Ignacio Sánchez Mejías,
whom Lorca would, seven years later, further immor-
talize as the subject of his famous poem "Lament for the
Death of a Bullfighter." The poets who attended formed
the nucleus of the literary phenomenon that was to be
known as "the generation of 1927": Lorca, Rafael Alberti, Jorge Guillén, José Bergamín, Gerardo Diego,
Damaso Alonso, and Juan Chabás. (Other poets usually
grouped in that generation, all of whom were—or became—friends of Lorca, are: Pedro Salinas, Vicente
Aleixandre, Luis Cernuda, Emilio Prados, and Manuel
Altolaguirre.) At that gathering in Seville, it was Lorca
who won the greatest public acclaim. Rafael Alberti
later recalled that in its enthusiasm for Lorca's poems
from the yet unpublished *Gypsy Ballad (Romancero gi-*

*tano)* the audience not only waved handkerchiefs and threw their hats in the air, but also—the highest possible accolade—threw their suit jackets.[34] One young poet, Adriano del Valle, was so carried away that he climbed on a chair and threw his tie and collar as well.[35] After the evening presentations, the poets drank together in the cabarets or sang and danced in the streets of Seville until dawn.

After his successes in Barcelona and Seville, Lorca felt restless in Granada's artistically unadventurous climate. He and several friends had often joked about the conservative or bourgeois attitudes toward art held by *los putrefactos* ("the putrified ones") of Granada and had planned for over a year to launch an avant-garde literary review that would jolt their complacency. The first issue of *Cock (Gallo)* appeared on March 9, 1928. Its twenty-two oversized pages included Lorca's introductory satirical prose piece "The Story of this Cock," as well as contributions by Jorge Guillén, Melchor Fernández Almagro, José Bergamín, and Salvador Dalí. Lorca's delight with its reception is evident in a letter he wrote to Sebastian Gasch:

Cock was a perfect scandal in Granada. Granada is a literary city and never has anything *new* occurred in it. That's why Cock caused a furor you cannot imagine. The issue sold out in two days and today they are paying double for copies. At the university yesterday there was a big fight between the pro-cocks and the anti-cocks, and in cafés, clubs, and houses it's the only topic of conversation.[36]

Within the month, as if to prove that the perpetrators of *Cock* did not take themselves too seriously, *Turkey (Pavo)* appeared. This was a four-page, mimeographed pastiche of the parent journal,[37] and it contained the following statement of purpose:

This periodical appears to imitate a certain journal that claims to be of Granada, but those young men must not think that

they are the only cause of the appearance of this turkey. . . .
The aforementioned journal greets imaginary colleagues with
a few cock-a-doodle-doos. . . . We cannot respond with the
same song, since nature has endowed us with another very
distinctive one; and so, therefore, we put our finger in our
mouth and go "gobble-gobble."[38]

The second and last issue of *Cock* came out in
April. Its lead article was a piece about Picasso by Sebastian Gasch. Among its other offerings were an ex-
cerpt of a novel by Lorca's brother Francisco, and two
of Lorca's very short plays written in quasi-cinematic
style: *The Virgin, the Sailor, and the Student (La Doncella, el marinero y el estudiante)* and *Buster Keaton's
Stroll (El Paseo de Buster Keaton)*. An antiartistic mani-
festo, signed by Dalí, Gasch, and Luis Montanya, inspired by the manifestoes of surrealism that had been
issued in Paris during the preceding four years, was the
most outrageous feature of this issue. The projected
third issue of *Cock* never appeared, perhaps because of
financial constraints, or literary jealousies, or disap-
pointment about the journal's limited impact on Granada's staid intellectuals.

*Gypsy Ballad (Romancero gitano)*, written between 1924 and 1927, and published in July 1928, was
an unprecedented success. These poems—especially
"The Faithless Wife," "The Ballad of the Spanish Civil
Guard," and "The Death of Antonito el Camborio"
—were recited everywhere and made Lorca the most
popular poet in Spain. That sudden, unexpected fame
coincided with the beginning of a period of severe emotional disturbance that altered Lorca's normally ebul-
liant personality. His depression lingered, varying in
intensity, during the following year. He was somewhat
bothered by the public's assumption that, dark com-
plexioned as he was, he must be of gypsy descent; his
frequent denials in letters and interviews were emphatic: "Gypsies are a theme. Nothing more. I would

be the same poet if I wrote about sewing needles or hydraulic landscapes. Besides, the gypsy myth makes me sound like an uncultured, uneducated *primitive poet,* which you well know I am not."[39] In the same letter, to Jorge Guillén, he mentioned what anguish it caused him to see some of the poems from *Gypsy Ballad* published in the periodical *Litoral* with more than ten gross errors that completely undermined the poetry. To Jorge Zalamea he wrote, "I enclose some unpublished verses, the feelings of a friend and a man, which I would not wish to make public. I want and must have my privacy. If I fear *stupid fame* it is precisely for that reason. The famous man knows the bitterness of having his heart coldly exposed by the dark lanterns that *others* shine at it."[40]

Lorca's emotional crisis had deeper causes than the consequences of success. In Spain at that period, sexuality was not a subject open to discussion, although Spanish poetry could be passionately sensuous. Marcelle Auclair reports that she knew Lorca for many years without ever suspecting that he was a homosexual.[41] Even long after Lorca's death, his friends never put in writing any more than an oblique reference to his "defect." One factor contributing to Lorca's depression in 1928 may have been anxiety over rumors of his homosexuality, fueled by some in Granada who had taken offense at *Cock;* he dreaded the possibility that his parents or Falla or Fernando de los Ríos might learn his secret.[42] Not until the early 1930s, apparently, could Lorca feel truly reconciled to his own homosexuality. The anguish it caused him before that is obvious in his letters to Adriano del Valle:

I am a poor passionate and silent fellow, who—rather like the marvelous Verlaine—carries inside himself a lily that cannot be watered, and to the simple eyes that look at me I show a rose reddened with the sexual shading of the April peony, which is not my heart's truth. . . . I see many problems ahead of me, many eyes imprisoning me, many nervous battles between head and heart. . . . Each passing day brings me a new doubt and new sadness. Sadness over the enigma that I am. There is in us, friend Adriano, a desire for love without suffering and for innate goodness, but the exterior force of temptation and the overwhelming tragedy of physiology undertake to destroy it. . . . Why should one struggle against the flesh when there is the frightful problem of the spirit to be faced?. . . . I am quite romantic and that is my greatest pride. In a century of zeppelins and stupid deaths, I sob at my piano dreaming of a Handelian mist and I make verses that are very much my own, singing to Christ and Buddha and Mahomet and Pan alike. I have my piano as a lyre and in place of ink I have the sweat of desire, the yellow pollen of my interior lily and my great love.[43]

Lorca's extant references to whatever was specifically troubling him in the summer of 1928 occur largely in his letters to Jorge Zalamea:

At the moment I have a kind of poetry to OPEN THE VEINS, a poetry EVADING reality with an emotion that reflects all my love for things and my mockery of things. Love of dying and ridicule of dying. Love. My heart. So it is. . . . One must be happy, it's a *duty* to be happy. You I will tell that I am going through one of the saddest and most difficult periods of my life.[44]

Lorca struggled consciously to overcome his sadness, and he turned to God:

These last few days I have *resolved* by an act of the will one of the most sorrowful states I've ever been in. You cannot imagine what it is to spend entire nights on the balcony, to look out at a nocturnal Granada that is *empty* for me, and not to find the slightest consolation in anything. Well, then . . . you must be on your guard against letting your state of being infiltrate your poetry, because it will betray you by opening up what is purest in you to the inspection of those who ought *never* to see it. That's why I'm disciplining myself now to write these *academic* analyses and I open my soul to the sym-

bol of the Holy Sacrament and my eroticism in the "Ode to
Sesostris," which is half finished.[45]

The "Ode to the Holy Sacrament of the Altar," 1928, is
one of very few religious poems in Lorca's entire work,
but careful investigation by José Luis Vila-San-Juan has
revealed that during Holy week, in 1929, disguised in a
hooded penitential robe, Lorca carried the cross at the
head of the procession of penitents in Granada, and on
May 20 of that year, he was inscribed as an active member of the religious brotherhood, the Cofradía de Santa
María de la Alhambra.[46]
     What Lorca called his "sentimental crisis" was
compounded, if not partially caused, by the break in his
relationship with Dalí. Dalí's guest at his family's
homes in Cadaqués and Figueras that summer of 1928
was not Lorca, but Luis Buñuel, with whom Dalí would
soon collaborate on the shocking silent film *An Andalusian Dog (Un Chien andalou,* 1929). What was probably
Dalí's last letter to Lorca (cited in its entirety in Antonina Rodrigo's *García Lorca en Cataluña)* criticized
Lorca's just-published *Gypsy Ballad* for being too traditional; in essence, Dalí was reproaching Lorca for not
having jumped on the surrealist bandwagon. In a letter
to Gasch dated September 8, 1928, Lorca referred to
Dalí's "sharp and arbitrary letter that sets up an interesting poetic dispute," and he added: "Don't forget to
encourage Dalí to come to Granada. We need to see
each other for many reasons."[47] Apparently, Lorca did
not see Dalí before the latter left in December for
Paris, where he met Gala, whom he later married.
     The loss of Dalí was counterbalanced by Lorca's
new friendship with Carlos and Bebé Morla Lynch, the
Chilean Ambassador and his charming wife, to whom
Lorca was introduced in March 1929. A deep, mutual
affection developed rapidly, and Lorca visited them
daily in their home whenever he was in Madrid. There,

spellbinding and radiant, he would sing and play the piano until 3:00 A.M. and then apologize for leaving early. When he was away from Madrid his letters expressed how much he felt at ease with the Morlas—free to weep, to exult, to be tender or silly. One example will suffice, from a letter written in August 1931:

On September 15 or 20 I will be in Madrid, so it's less than a month until we are together again in your house, something I ardently anticipate; it seems like the best thing that could happen to me.

I adore Bebé. I love her so much, and she will never know how many thousands of snapshots of her activities and her divine poses I keep in my imagination. Dresses, gestures, words, and even the run in her stocking she had one day, I recall with tenderness.

I also have great fondness for your bathroom, although nobody else feels that way about such rooms since nobody wants to speak of them; nevertheless, I felt quite at home stretched out in your bathtub while you combed your hair and Carlitos [the Morlas' son] smeared pomade on his, and Bebé called "Come and eat!"[48]

The Morlas understood the suffering caused by Lorca's "sentimental penumbra" and encouraged him to accept Fernando de los Ríos's invitation to accompany him to New York in June 1929. Don Fernando, who was to lecture at the New School for Social Research, persuaded Lorca's parents to provide financial support for the trip that was intended to broaden Lorca's horizons. Lorca's activities in New York have been painstakingly documented by Daniel Eisenberg.[49] Lorca moved into Room 617 of the dormitory Furnald Hall at Columbia University and enrolled in a summer course for educated foreigners who knew no English. Miss Amy I. Shaw (later Mrs. Allen Abbott), who taught the course, recalled that Lorca attended regularly and that her students were expected to master a three-hundred-word vocabulary and simple grammatical constructions

in English. However, those who knew Lorca at that
time claim that he learned very little English during his
nine months in the United States. The cultural disorientation he felt, complicated by the language barrier, is
evident in such poems as "Landscape of the Vomiting
Multitude," "Landscape of the Urinating Multitude,"
and "Christmas on the Hudson," which were later collected, along with poems expressing a spiritual kinship
with the blacks he saw on a number of visits to Harlem,
in *Poet in New York (Poeta en Nueva York,* 1940).

At the end of the summer session, Lorca visited an
American friend, Philip Cummings, at Lake Eden Mills
in Vermont. That ten-day retreat to the green, moun-
tainous countryside—best recounted by another of
Lorca's American friends, Mildred Adams, in her 1977
book *García Lorca: Playwright and Poet*—inspired
such melancholy poems as "Double Poem of Lake
Eden" and "Little Boy Stanton" in *Poet in New York.*
Lorca also visited in the homes of two Columbia University professors of Spanish literature with whom he
had become friends, Federico de Onís and Angel del
Río. In the fall, Lorca again enrolled at Columbia University, but soon withdrew from classes. He preferred
to spend his time writing, walking about the city, and
visiting with Spanish-speaking friends like fellow-stu-
dents John Crow and Francis Hayes, Mexican painter
Emilio Amero, publisher Herschel Brickell, and poet
León Felipe, who translated Walt Whitman into Spanish. He had a joyous reunion with dancers La Argentina
(Antonia Mercé) and La Argentinita (Encaración López
Júlvez), both of whom performed in New York that winter, and with Ignacio Sánchez Mejías, whose lecture on
"The Pass of Death" at the Spanish Institute Lorca introduced. He wrote a silent-film scenario, *Trip to the
Moon (Viaje a la luna),* and more poetry, including his
second religious poem, "Crucifixion." He reportedly
witnessed six suicides when the stock market crashed

on October 29, 1929. He spent Christmas Eve at the apartment of Herschel and Norma Brickell, and was taken to midnight mass at St. Paul the Apostle Church and then to a Childs Restaurant on Columbus Circle for hotcakes and maple syrup.[50] He lectured on Spanish song at Vassar College and on poetry at Columbia University, and accepted a sudden invitation to give a series of lectures in Cuba. He arrived in Havana on March 7, 1930.

"I left New York with a feeling of profound admiration. I had found many friends there and I took away the most useful experience of my life," he later recalled in a lecture, "A Poet in New York," which he frequently gave between 1931 and 1935. "But the boat took me away from that and carried me toward the perfumes of cinnamon and palm emanating from the America that has roots, God's America, Spanish America."[51] Warmly received, he spent three months in Cuba, lecturing frequently and enjoying the reimmersion in Hispanic culture. His renewed exuberance may be sensed in the bright images and lively rhythms of his poem "I'll Go to Santiago." At the same time he began writing on the letterhead stationery of Havana's Hotel La Union his wildly unconventional and daringly self-revealing play *The Audience (El Público)*, which was completed that year but not published until 1976.

On Lorca's return from Cuba to Spain, his ship docked for one day in New York, but he was not allowed ashore since his visa had expired. The Brickells and music critic Olin Downes joined him for a farewell shipboard luncheon. According to the Brickells, he had gained too much weight in Cuba[52] and had become "wholly male, and very vulgar."[53] Another strong reaction was provoked by Lorca's reading of *The Audience* in the Morla Lynch home on his return to Spain. Disturbed by its violence and homosexuality, Bebé Morla begged him not to try to have it staged.[54] When Lorca and Rafael Martínez Nadal left the stunned gathering, Lorca told him: "Either they've grasped nothing or they were afraid, and I sympathize with them. The play is most difficult and for the time being impossible to put on. But in ten or twenty years it will be a great success. You'll see."[55]

Lorca had returned to Spain at a time of political tension and uncertainty. However, the general elections of April 12, 1931, which resulted in the proclamation of the Second Republic (replacing a monarchy propped up by a prime minister with dictatorial powers), ushered in a period of general optimism. The new government initiated a number of social reforms among which was the creation of a Ministry of Culture and Public Information headed by Don Fernando de los Ríos. Lorca—noting that peasants and workers flocked to the Prado Museum now open on Sundays, and recalling the melancholy emptiness of the Spanish villages he had visited in 1916–1917 and in 1922, and perhaps even inspired by the itinerant puppet shows that had enriched his childhood—conceived a project for taking classical Spanish theatre to those people in their villages. The touring theatre company, composed of unpaid university students, would be called *La Barraca* or "hut" to create the image of a "little house on wheels" for the truckful of scenery and props. Lorca's enthusiasm quickly captured the imaginations of many. Mildred Adams published a story on the proposed endeavor in *Theatre Arts Monthly* in March 1932, the same month in which it won official approval under the sponsorship of Don Fernando de los Ríos.

Lorca served as artistic director of *La Barraca* in close collaboration with Eduardo Ugarte, who was also much loved by the company. *La Barraca*'s insignia was a comic mask centered on a spoked wheel. Every aspect of production drew Lorca's attention: he respectfully cut and adapted plays by Lope de Vega, Cer-

vantes, and Calderón for modern audiences: he worked
with the actors in rehearsal, contributed to the design
and construction of scenery and costumes, helped load
the truck and set up lights, and, briefly, acted a small
role.[56] Because the original troupe of thirty performers
and technicians included eight women, an elderly chap-
erone was hired to safeguard the reputations of the
younger women, but that concession to prevailing mo-
res was eventually dropped.[57]

After the successful premiere in the square in front
of the cathedral in the medieval town of Burgo de Osma
on July 10, 1932, Lorca often traveled with the company. He would study the reactions of the simple, un-
tutored village audiences and then tighten the script or
adjust the staging on the basis of what he observed.[58]
Without that experience he might not have achieved
the transition from pure poetry to the theatre poetry of
his last plays. He assured an interviewer that the practi-
cal work was not a distraction from his writing: "It all
comes down to the joy of creating, of doing things. Besides, my work on *La Barraca* is a great education. I've
learned so much. Now I really feel like a director."[59]
Another 1934 interview reveals still more clearly the
theatre's lure for him and the importance he attached to
it: "*La Barraca* is to me my whole creative effort, the
work that interests me, that now beguiles me more
than my literary work. For *La Barraca*, for example,
I've often left off writing a verse or finishing a play
(*Yerma* is one of them) which I would have finished already if I had not interrupted myself to get back to the
Spanish countryside, on one of those marvelous excur-
sions of 'my theatre.'"[60] Amazingly, Lorca did manage
to write a great deal during that period, including his
"Six Galician Poems," "Lament for Ignacio Sánchez
Mejías," the poems that would be published in 1936 as
*Diván of the Tamarit, Blood Wedding,* the lost play *The
Destruction of Sodom,* revisions of *When Five Years*

*Pass, The Shoemaker's Prodigious Wife, Don Cristo-
bal's Puppet Theatre,* and *The Love of Don Perlimplin
with Belisa in the Garden,* as well as his adaptations of
Spanish Golden Age plays.

During the four years of its existence, *La Barraca*
brought thirteen different productions[61] to seventy-
four villages and towns in every part of Spain.[62] It survived several changes in government and even the loss
of half of its subsidy after the elections of 1934, but finally came to an end in April 1936 in the face of rapidly
escalating political, social, and economic disorders. *La
Barraca's* success in raising the cultural level of rural
Spaniards cannot be measured, but theatre historians
agree that it had a lasting influence on post–Civil War
Spanish theatre in helping to realize Lorca's goal of
ridding the Spanish stage of "false sirens, . . . sawdust
hearts, and superficial dialogue" and giving it a theatre
that would "capture the social pulse, the historical
pulse, the drama of its people, and the true color of
their countryside and spirit."[63]

Lorca's importance as a dramatist caught up with
his fame as a poet in the last three years of his life. His
period of greatest triumph in the theatre began with
the production of *Blood Wedding (Bodas de sangre)* by
the company of Josefina Díaz de Artigas at the Beatriz
Theatre in Madrid on March 8, 1933. This first of
Lorca's three great tragedies of Spanish womanhood
was inspired by a newspaper story he had read in 1928,
and it was written in a single week in 1932. Directed by
Lorca himself and designed by Santiago Ontañon,
*Blood Wedding* overwhelmed its sophisticated opening-
night audience with its stunning combination of ele-
mental passions, rural realism, and poetic symbolism.
The storm of applause, rave reviews, substantial run,
and subsequent productions in other cities were indica-
tions that at last Lorca was to be financially indepen-
dent of his parents.

Within a month, on April 5, another play by Lorca
had its successful premiere in Madrid. This was *The
Love of Don Perlimplín with Belisa in the Garden (El
Amor de Don Perlimplín con Belisa en el jardín)*, which
had been prohibited from production in 1929 because
of its suggestive subtitle, "An Erotic Alleluia." The
story of an old man cuckolded by his young wife may
also have been personally offensive to the sixty-year-old
dictator Miguel Primo de Rivera. Its 1933 production
was directed by Pura de Ucelay, a wealthy Madrid society woman who, in order to encourage productions of
plays rejected by commercial theatres, created theatre
clubs like the Club Anfistora that presented *Don Perlimplín* at the Eslava Theatre along with the early, short
version of *The Shoemaker's Prodigious Wife* that had
been written in 1926 and previously produced in 1930.

In October Lorca made his second and last trip
abroad. He accepted an invitation to lecture and attend
productions of his plays in Buenos Aires. There he saw
*Blood Wedding, Mariana Pineda,* and the premiere of
his expanded version of *The Shoemaker's Prodigious
Wife*, all produced by Lola Membrives's company. His
adaptation of Lope de Vega's *The Silly Lady (La Dama
boba)*, for which Lorca composed and arranged music,
presented by Eva Franco's company, was reportedly
seen by sixty thousand spectators.[64] Lorca's reception
in South America was quite the opposite of his lonely
stay in New York; the public outpouring of affection and
appreciation continued throughout his busy five-and-
one-half-month visit. He escaped the constant round of
festivities in Buenos Aires for two weeks in February
1934 by going to Montevideo, Uruguay, where he
hoped to find time to work on *Yerma,* but there too he
gave lectures and enjoyed the city's social and literary
life. In March he was honored jointly with Chilean poet
Pablo Neruda at a banquet sponsored by the P.E.N.
Club of Buenos Aires; his friendship with Neruda

would be renewed the following year when Neruda came to Madrid. At a reception just before his return to Spain, Lorca received unexpected homage: representatives from several Latin American republics proclaimed him "ambassador of Spanish culture to Latin America." According to Suzanne Byrd, "Lorca's popularity in Buenos Aires had a significant influence upon commerce and diplomacy between Argentina and Spain."[65]

In Spain Lorca resumed his activities with *La Barraca*, his frequent lectures and recitations, and, as always, his enjoyment of many hours each day spent with friends. Upon the completion of *Yerma*, he read it to his friends at the Morla Lynch home, and the play opened at the Español Theatre in Madrid on December 29, 1934, performed by Margarita Xirgu's company under the direction of Cipriano Rivas Cherif. The worsening political climate caused apprehension about the opening, especially since Margarita Xirgu, who played the title role did not hide her liaison with Manuel Azaña, a leader in Spain's still-shaky Republican government, who had been accused of fomenting strikes and revolutionary activities in Catalonia. Such considerations were forgotten, however, as the audience came under the spell of Lorca's powerful tragic poem. *Yerma*'s success was even greater than that of *Blood Wedding*. Realizing the importance of this play in the development of modern Spanish theatre, Madrid's actors and actresses petitioned for a special late-night performance that they could attend after their own evening performances. At that occasion, on February 2, 1935, Lorca gave his famous "Talk about the Theatre," in which he expressed his artistic credo and his vision of a theatre that would not give in to the temptations of commercialism, but which would keep aloft its artistic ideals by means of discipline, sacrifice, and love.[66] At the one-hundredth performance of *Yerma*, on March

12, Lorca read, for the first time in public, his "Lament for Ignacio Sánchez Mejías."

Lorca accompanied Margarita Xirgu's company to Catalonia for the equally triumphal Barcelona premiere of *Yerma* on September 17, and he remained there for most of the next three months. The last major Lorca premiere during his lifetime was that of *Doña Rosita the Spinster* at Barcelona's Principal Palace on December 12, 1935. Again Lorca's favorite actress, Margarita Xirgu, performed the title role, directed by Cipriano Rivas Cherif, with settings by Lorca's friend Manuel Fontanals. This bittersweet comedy was favorably reviewed and ran for forty-two performances.

Lorca worked on a number of plays in 1936, but only *The House of Bernarda Alba* is known to have been completed; its posthumous premiere was given by Margarita Xirgu's company on March 8, 1945, in Buenos Aires. Among the plays in progress that have been missing since Lorca's death are: *The Sacrifice of Iphigenia*, written in 1927; *The Destruction of Sodom*, apparently completed in January 1935; *The Daughters of Lot*, which may have been an alternate title for *The Destruction of Sodom* and would have been part of a biblical trilogy with his projected *Cain and Abel* and *Thamar and Amnon; Blackballed (La Bola negra)*, a homosexual tragedy; *Blood Has No Voice (La Sangre no tinene voz)*, a play about incest; *The Beautiful Beast (La Bestia hermosa)*, first mentioned by Lorca in 1931; and *Dreams of My Cousin Aurelia (Los Sueños de mi prima Aurelia)*, an Andalusian comedy. Lorca's lost poetry, *Sonnets of Dark Love (Sonetas del amor oscuro)*, was a group of about forty poems on themes of masculine intimacy; Lorca gave the manuscript for safekeeping to Rafael Rapún, who was killed in the Civil War.

The death of Lorca's friend Ignacio Sánchez Mejías on August 13, 1934, of wounds inflicted by a bull named Granadino de Ayala during the great *torero*'s fourth *corrida* after a seven-year absence from the bullring, seemed to call up in Lorca, along with his profound grief, a premonition of his own death. He told Marcelle Auclair:

Everything was destined; inescapable fate. I foresaw it all from the moment Ignacio told me of his decision to return to bullfighting. . . . Strangely, I'm not revolted. Ignacio's death is like my death, an apprenticeship for my own death. I feel a peace that astonishes me. Perhaps because I have been intuitively warned? There are moments in which I push my vision of Ignacio's corpse to the point of imagining it destroyed, torn to shreds by worms and brambles. Finally I encounter a silence that is not nothingness, but mystery.[67]

Lorca's death, like that of Sánchez Mejías, had a fatalistic aura about it. In making choices—like his decision to return to Granada—that should have afforded him safety and time to write, Lorca moved steadily closer to his own death. Afterward, an official silence about the circumstances of his death lasted for many years in Spain, compounded by fear that prevented others from speaking. What is now known about the subject is due largely to the persistent efforts of Marcelle Auclair and of Irish scholar Ian Gibson. Working independently of each other, they carefully sifted the evidence of documents, public statements, private interviews, and inquiries tracing every possible lead. Ian Gibson devoted fourteen years to this research, and his two books—*The Death of Lorca* (1973) and *Granada en 1936 y el asesinato de Federico García Lorca* (1979)— remain the most authoritative studies of the subject.

Lorca's last day in Madrid, July 16, 1936, has been chronicled by Rafael Martínez Nadal, who lunched with Lorca and saw him off on the train to Granada that night. Since February, Spain had been plagued with strikes and outbursts of violence. Lorca had rejected opportunities to return to South America or New York, to go to Mexico, or to stay with friends on the coast of Spain, but he was also frightened of remaining in the capital, where the sound of gunfire in the streets was no longer uncommon. Furthermore, he sensed that it was not a propitious moment to present a difficult play like *When Five Years Pass* (*Así que pasen cinco años*), which the Club Anfistora had been rehearsing for a July opening; he asked that it be postponed until the fall. After long indecision he made up his mind on July 16 to return to his parents' home in Granada to celebrate his father's and his own saint's name day.

On Saint Federico's Day, July 18, civil war broke out in Spain, precipitated by the military uprising led by General Francisco Franco at Melilla in Spanish Morocco. Andalusia was the first region to fall to the Nationalist Movement, and reprisals against those who favored the Republic were particularly brutal and far-reaching in Granada. Gibson estimates that over forty-five hundred executions took place in Granada between 1936 and 1940 as part of the Nationalist repression. Lorca's brother-in-law, Manuel Fernández Montesinos, who only a month before had been elected mayor of Granada, was arrested on August 3 and executed on August 16. Lorca's presence at the family home, Huerta de San Vicente, was known, and it became clear that he could not safely remain there. Lorca found refuge on August 9 in the home of his friend Luís Rosales Camacho, a young poet, whose brothers were prominent members of the Falange. The Rosales family welcomed Lorca as a friend and a guest, and it was thought that their political affiliation would allay any suspicion of his whereabouts.

Lorca's family had outspokenly expressed sympathy for the Popular Front, and their close friendship with liberal thinker Fernando de los Ríos was well known. There is no doubt that Lorca too was antifascist. His last works indicate increasing willingness to treat

social issues in art, and the liberal or socialist drift of his
thinking is documented in Gibson's second book. However, it also remains clear that Lorca never aligned
himself with any single political group or party. Only a
month before his death, for example, Lorca told Damaso Alonso: "I will never be political. I am a revolutionary because there are no true poets that are not
revolutionaries. Don't you agree? But political, I will
never, never be!"[68] When asked about his political
preference, he would habitually answer: "I am on the
side of the poor." Just before leaving Madrid, he told
Edgar Neville: "I'm going, because here they keep mixing me up with politics, which I don't understand, nor
do I want to know anything. . . . I am everybody's
friend, and all I want is for everybody to be able to eat
and work."[69]

For Lorca, friendship had no political boundaries.
His friend Rafael Alberti had gone to the USSR and returned a communist, yet it was as natural for Lorca to
participate in a tribute to Alberti's poetry (on February
9, 1936) as it was for him to discuss poetry with Falangist leader José Antonio Primo de Rivera[70] or to be a
guest in a Falangist household. In his last interview,
Lorca told Luís Bagaría:

I am totally Spanish and it would be impossible for me to live
outside my geographical boundaries; but I hate whatever is
Spanish just for the sake of being Spanish and nothing else. I
am a brother to all men and I detest anyone who sacrifices
himself for an abstract nationalist idea only because he loves
his country with a blindfold on his eyes. A good Chinese is
closer to me than a bad Spaniard. I sing of Spain and feel
Spain in the marrow of my bones, but above all I am a citizen
of the world and brother to all.[71]

In the same interview Lorca expressed the attitude that
was probably as much responsible for any hostility toward him in Granada as any political labels that may
have been pinned on him: The fall of Moorish Granada

to Catholic Ferdinand and Isabella in 1492 "was a disastrous event, although they teach the contrary in schools. An admirable brand of civilization, of poetry, of astronomy, of architecture, and a delicacy unique in the world—all were lost, to be replaced by a poor, craven town, a 'wasteland' now dominated by the worst bourgeoisie in Spain."[72] In such a town it is hardly surprising that the homosexual poet who had published *Cock* in 1928 would be vulnerable during Granada's reign of terror when the infamous "black squads" rounded up victims on the slightest pretext.

On August 16, Lorca was arrested at the Rosales home by Ramón Ruíz Alonso and others. He was taken to the Civil Government in Granada where he was held for three days. Despite efforts by his parents, Luís Rosales, and Manuel de Falla to gain his release, he was seen only by the Montesinos's family servant Angelina, who took food to his cell on the mornings of August 17 and 18. On the third day, his cell was empty. During the preceding night, on orders from the civil governor, José Valdés Guzmán, he had been taken outside town in a car with one other victim, a one-legged village schoolteacher named Dióscuro Galindo González. On the road outside the tiny village of Viznár, not far from an ancient Moorish spring called Ainadamar or Fuente Granda, the two men were shot and buried in a common unmarked grave in a grove of olive trees.

Since 1936 Lorca's international reputation has continued to grow. In Spain, despite a twenty-four-year hiatus in the production of his plays, his memory was kept alive just as his poems had lived in the hearts and minds of people even before their publication. The wish expressed in "Gacela of Dark Death" from *Diván of the Tamarit* (1936) may be considered fulfilled:

> I want to sleep a little while,
> a little while, a minute, a century,
> but let everyone know that I have not died . . .

*Quiero dormir un rato,*
*un rato, un minuto, un siglo;*
*pero que todos sepan que no he muerto . . .*[73]

His remarkable achievement of total artistry is exqui-
sitely summed up by his friend, guitarist Regino Sainz
de la Maza:

He was a stimulus. A privileged being. It's hard to understand how he captured, how he was in tune with all the artistic currents of his time, without having traveled widely. He
was an integral artist, attracted to everything. He could have
been a genius as a musician, as a painter; he saw everything
as a kind of poetry. Those prodigious harmonizations of popular songs that he did without having studied harmony were a
marvel, a work of pure instinct. His humanity was extraordi-
nary, capable of bringing out whatever was good in a person,
things that a person might never have thought possible except
in his presence.[74]

# 2

**The Key "Unperformable Plays"**

The publication in 1976 of Lorca's long-suppressed play *The Audience (El Público,* written in 1930) has shed new light on preoccupations underlying all Lorca's later work. The play's seemingly uncharacteristic form and content contradict the usual notions of Lorca as an Andalusia-centered lyrical poet or as a dramatist concerned primarily with the tragic plight of Spanish womanhood. *The Audience* was not an aberration in Lorca's development. It heralded a new direction that his most serious efforts were to take, even as he continued to write the better-known works that were instantly popular with general audiences.

In a 1931 interview, Lorca declared: "The new theatre, avant-garde in form and theory, is my major preoccupation. New York is the only place for taking the pulse of a new art of the theatre."[1] Hostile as that alien culture had seemed to him, New York unleashed certain creative impulses that produced the arcane and violent poems of his *Poet in New York* as well as several plays that Lorca called "unperformable." In her essay "Poet and Public" in *Europe* (August-September 1980), Marie Laffranque points out clear correspondences between *Poet in New York* and *The Audience,* including Lorca's new emphasis on social concerns and his preoccupation with the theme of homosexual love. (The poems will be discussed in chapter 6.)

Besides *The Audience,* two other "unperformable" pieces have survived: the relatively neglected *When Five Years Pass (Así que pasen cinco años,* written in 1931) and the first act of a projected three-act play that was published in 1978 as *Play without a Title (Comedia sin título).* The most accessible of the three "unperformable plays," *When Five Years Pass,* was scheduled for performance by the Club Anfistora in April 1936, but Lorca felt that the atmosphere of political uncertainty in Madrid was not propitious for the production of so experimental a work, and he asked that it be withdrawn—with the result that it was not performed in his lifetime.

*Play without a Title,* which is strikingly similar in many ways to the two earlier "unperformable plays," was not written until December 1935 or January 1936. In the nearly five-year interval between *When Five Years Pass* and *Play without a Title,* Lorca wrote *Blood Wedding* (1932), *Yerma* (1934), and *Doña Rosita the Spinster* (1935), but he stated in an interview (*La Voz,* April 7, 1936) that it was in his "impossible plays" that his "true subject matter" might be found. "However," he continued, "in order to present an image and be respected, I have done other things."[2] Citing Lorca's need to consolidate his professional position, Miguel García-Posada calls the plays written between 1932 and 1936 "the fruit of a tacit compromise" with the requirements of commercial theatre; the existence of *Play without a Title* is evidence that Lorca did not abandon his "true subject matter" during those years.[3]

It is apparent that Lorca sublimated his personal preoccupations in the three great tragedies about women: *Blood Wedding, Yerma,* and *House of Bernarda Alba* (1936). His poetic treatment of the anguish of the barren wife in *Yerma,* for example, masks the anguish of the homosexual who knows he will never have children. The repressive societal conventions that weigh upon Bernarda Alba's claustrophobic household are analogous to the rigid mold imposed upon the theatre by Spain's middle classes, which Lorca wished to break. Difficult as it is to penetrate and interpret the very personal imagery, symbolism, and anecdotal references in the "unperformable plays," their "true subject matter" may serve to illuminate the subtexts of Lorca's better-known plays. For that reason, and because relatively little has yet been written about *The Audience* and *Play without a Title,* which have only recently become available, this chapter will analyze them in some detail, along with *When Five Years Pass.*

Scene 1 of *The Audience* is set in the Theatre Director's office. There is a large print of a hand on one of the blue walls of the set, and the windows are X-ray plates. Miguel García-Posada sees the setting as one of several clues to suggest that the entire play takes place in the mind of the Director.[4] Without discounting that possibility, one might also interpret the setting to mean that the play has both cosmic and psychological dimensions: the blue walls and handprint evoke infinity and the hand of God or destiny, and X-rays are a means of probing the internal workings of man.

A Servant tells the Director that "the audience is out there," and he replies: "Let them in." However, the Director is upset by the entrance of Four White Horses, each carrying a long golden trumpet; (the play abounds with many such obvious phallic symbols). The Horses remind the Director of past intimacies, but he sends them away, insisting that he runs an "open-air theatre." His next visitors are three Men With Black Beards, identically dressed in swallow-tailed coats. They congratulate the Director on his latest work, *Romeo and Juliet,* but hint that there is more to the title characters than meets the eye. Man 1 (who is also called Gonzalo) appeals to the Director (who is also called Enrique) to reveal the truth behind appearances.

Romeo and Juliet appear to be a man and woman in love, but the "poisonous flower" of love[5] would exercise its power over them even if Romeo were a bird and Juliet a stone, or if Romeo were a grain of salt and Juliet a map. Man 1 prophesies: "We will have to bury the theatre because of general cowardice. And I will have to shoot myself. . . . I will have to shoot myself in order to inaugurate the true theatre, the theatre under the sand."

Fearfully, the Director replies:

What do I do with the audience if I remove the railings from the bridge? The mask would come and devour me. Once I saw a man devoured by the mask. The strongest youths in the city were stuffing great wads of old newspapers in its rump with blood-stained pikes. And there was the time in America when the mask hanged a boy by his own intestines.[6]

The mask clearly represents societal convention and accepted morality, which the Director does not wish to antagonize. The men press the issue of representing the truth on stage. The Director calls for Elena. Man 1 retaliates by calling for the Four Horses to return and take roles in the play.

The Men place a screen at stage center and push the Director behind it. He reappears at the other end as a boy dressed in white satin with a white ruff at the neck. In *The Audience* and in his filmscript *A Trip to the Moon,* Lorca refers to this outfit as a "White Harlequin Costume," although he must have envisioned what we would call a Pedrolino or Pierrot costume. Lorca specifies that with this transformation the role of the Director is taken by an actress. It is the first of several metamorphoses in *The Audience*.

The screen device apparently serves to bring out repressed facets of one's personality, for the Director then pushes Man 2 behind the screen and he emerges as a woman dressed in black pajama trousers with a crown of poppies, carrying a lorgnette with a blond mustache on it; when the character wishes to assume masculine authority she places the mustache in front of her mouth. Man 3 passes behind the screen and reappears without his beard, but wearing leather bracelets and carrying a whip. Man 1 does not undergo a transformation, perhaps because he—always open about his love for the Director—has no identity problem.

Elena enters. She, who "loved the Director very much when his theatre was in the open air," is dressed in a Greek garment and has feet of plaster. The name Elena, evoking Helen of Troy or idealized womanhood, suggests that she represents the Director's desire to force himself into a conventional heterosexual life style. Her classical costume may indicate that she is the muse who inspires the Director's work within safe, traditional artistic forms (like Lorca's more conventional plays).

The Servant (who passes behind the screen and is not transformed) leads Elena away. The others—Director, Three Men, and Four Horses—are now ready to begin the play.

Scene 2 is set in a "roman Ruin," which may be a scenic metaphor for antiquated theatre forms. There, a Figure Covered with Red Tendrils and a Figure Covered with Golden Harness Bells try to work out, through verbal transformations, the frustration of a physically impossible love:

FIGURE WITH BELLS: If I turned into a cloud?
FIGURE WITH TENDRILS: I would turn into an eye.
FIGURE WITH BELLS: If I turned into caca?
FIGURE WITH TENDRILS: I would turn into a fly.
FIGURE WITH BELLS: If I turned into an apple?
FIGURE WITH TENDRILS: I would turn into a kiss.
FIGURE WITH BELLS: If I turned into a breast?
FIGURE WITH TENDRILS: I would turn into a white sheet.
FIGURE WITH BELLS: And if I turned into a moonfish?
FIGURE WITH TENDRILS: I would turn into a knife.[7]

The metaphors of frustration proliferate as the two engage in a psychological battle, whose subtext is "Can you top this?" This sequence may be the attempt of one to dominate the other, as Martínez Nadal suggests,[8] or it is a series of boasts about how much one is willing to do for love of the other. Finally, the Figure with Tendrils blows a silver whistle. From the roof falls a child dressed in a red leotard, who announces: "The Emperor!"

The Roman Emperor enters with his Centurion, followed by the Four Horses with their trumpets. The Emperor picks up the child and carries it off into the ruins. Left with the two Figures, the Centurion pronounces "a curse on all your kind!" Because of their kind he is always on the road with the Emperor instead of remaining at home with his beautiful, prolific wife. A shriek is heard from behind the columns. The Emperor re-enters and removes black gloves, then red gloves, revealing his classically white hands. Unmistakably, the Emperor has murdered the innocent child in red. Marie Laffranque believes that the child represents an unborn infant who never has a chance to live;[9] by extending that interpretation, the child may symbolize the two Figures' unrealized love for each other —a love whose growth is prevented by convention-bound society.

The Emperor is searching for "one," and both Figures want to be that "one." The Emperor tells them: "One is one and always one. I've cut the throats of over forty boys who didn't want to say so."

CENTURION, *spitting:* One is one and only one.
EMPEROR: And there's no two.
CENTURION: Because if there were two the Emperor would not be searching high and low.[10]

The Figure with Tendrils slips off his costume and appears as a chalk-white nude. As the Emperor embraces him, the Figure with Tendrils offers to let the Emperor decapitate him "and leave my loving head in the ruin, the head of one who was always one." The Figure with Bells cries "Treason!," calls for Gonzalo, and pulls a screen out of a column. The Director and the three bearded Men enter from behind it. "He has betrayed us," the Figure with Bells tells the Director and Man 1 while the Emperor continues to embrace the Figure with Tendrils.

No single interpretation will suffice for the Roman Ruin scene. Since *pámpanos* means "vine leaves" as well as "tendrils," it is possible that Lorca intended the Figure with Tendrils, or Vine Leaves, to represent wine-drinking, while the Figure with Bells represents song and dance; symbiotically they create a bacchic revelry. Later scenes will offer clues that the Figure with Bells is one of the Director's personae and that the Figure with Tendrils is a persona of Man 1 (Gonzalo). The scene might then be their speculation about the consequences of attempting to express their unorthodox love within the restrictive format of neoclassicism. The willingness of the Figure with Tendrils to sacrifice himself for love is consistent with the characterization of Man 1, who never deviates in his love for the less constant Director. It is significant that when the Director and three Men enter at the end of the scene, the men have regained their beards; this suggests that their accusation of treason is made from a hypocritical point of view.

The Emperor, whose capriciousness and cruelty call up associations with Caligula, is not necessarily for or against homosexuals (although homosexuality is a possible referent for the "one" as opposed to heterosexuality or "two"). The Emperor's position of supremacy might symbolically align him with the force of destiny that arbitrarily assigns different sexual orientations to different human beings.

Lorca's familiarity with Freudian theory is certain,

since he referred to it in conversation and writing. Given that awareness, it is likely that the Emperor —whose authoritativeness functions like the disciplinarian sugerego in the human psyche and whose wanton cruelty is an eruption of the id or base instinct—in seeking "the one" is actually looking for an integrated personality, a balanced individual whose behavior is predominantly a function of the Freudian ego, the true self. We have seen that Man 1 is just such an integrated personality since he is not afraid to acknowledge his true nature.

These ideas seem to be borne out in Scene 3, which is played before a wall of sand. The Director and the three Men discuss a bloody fray that occurred in the presence of the Emperor. Man 1 says that both combatants could have won "by both being men and not letting themselves be sidetracked by false desires. By both being whole men. Can a man ever stop being a man?" The ideal of being "whole men" (egos) is posited in contrast to the opposing pulls of the id and the superego, an opposition that Man 1 likens to "marble forms flowing with secret desires beneath an impervious surface":

MAN 3: When the moon comes out, country children get together to defecate.
MAN 2: And behind the rushes, on the backwaters' cool bank, we found the track of the man who looks askance at the freedom of the naked.[11]

Man 1 volunteers to kill the Emperor and bring his head to the Director, who in turn would like to offer it as a gift to Elena. Her name provokes a fight between the Director and Man 1. Then Man 2 and Man 3 begin to fight. As soon as all have left the stage, the wall of sand opens to reveal Juliet's tomb in Verona. The setting is realistic, but Juliet, lying on her tomb, wears an opera costume with rosy celluloid breasts. She awakens

and speaks of her longing not for "mere discussions of
love or theatre," but for "loving."

White Horse 1 enters, sword in hand, and attempts to seduce Juliet, but she sees through the su-
perficiality of the love he offers: "It's all trickery—the
declaration of love, the broken mirror, the footprint in
water. Afterward you'll leave me in the tomb again, as
everyone does when they're trying to convince their listeners that true love is impossible." Later in the play
(Scene 5) it is revealed that Juliet is actually a boy doing
an Elizabethan-style interpretation of a feminine role.
That information may shed another light on the meaning of Juliet's dialogue with White Horse 1 in this
scene. White Horse 1 urges Juliet to let him carry her
out into the daylight, but she prefers the security of
night in her tomb. Thus, the opposition between a willingness to express one's homosexual nature openly (in
daylight) and a resigned acceptance of lonely solitude
without risk of censure (night) overlays the opposition
between promiscuousness and steadfastness in love.

A Black Horse enters. Wearing a crest of black
plumes and carrying a wheel in his hand, the Black
Horse speaks of "yearning in the blood and nausea from
the wheel." Three White Horses enter, carrying long
black lacquer canes. The Three White Horses want to
"go through Juliet's innards in order to achieve the resurrection of horses," but the Black Horse counsels her
against it. A stalemate exists between them when Man
1 and the Director enter. The Director is now in the
form of a White Harlequin.

MAN 1: Enough, gentlemen!
DIRECTOR: Open-air theatre!
WHITE HORSE 1: No. Now we have inaugurated the true thea-
tre, theatre under the sand.
*Black Horse:* To make known the truth about tombs.
THE THREE WHITE HORSES: Tombs with posters, footlights,
and long rows of orchestra seats.

MAN 1: Yes! We've already taken the first step. But I know
positively that three of you are hiding, that three of you still
swim on the surface. (*The three White Horses cluster together
worriedly*.) You're so accustomed to the coachman's whip and
the blacksmith's tongs, you're afraid of the truth.[12]

Rafael Martínez Nadal's interpretation of this difficult sequence focuses on the sepulchral setting and the
dialogue about resurrection; he associates the Black
Horse with death and the White Horse with new life,
which—Juliet is aware—contains the seeds of death
from the time of birth. Besides the biblical resonance of
that idea of resurrection from the tomb, one may also
extract from the sequence a comment on artistic creativity. The three White Horses, who have expressed a
preoccupation with form and are accused of "still
swimming on the surface," may represent intellectually
conceived art. This interpretation is reinforced by the
first White Horse's extolling of "ashes that form an apple;" for Lorca, the apple represented the consciousness that replaced innocence when Adam fell from
grace. Might resurrection through Juliet imply the
achievement of artistic viability by exploiting the work
of other artists like Shakespeare? Or may such a resurrection be seen as a way of attaining the oneiric status
of the Black Horse whose *duende* ("yearning in the
blood") is a deeper source of creativity than mere
awareness of form? We recall that *duende* is linked in
the Spanish consciousness with death. In his lecture on
*duende*, Lorca said that "*duende* does not come unless
it sees a possibility of death."[13]

In subsequent dialogue, a correlation is suggested
between form (or superficial technique) and the mask.
Man 1 declares that he has no mask, but that he must
struggle to tear the mask from the Director. The Director resists the embrace of Man 1 and they fight. The
Black Horse realizes that the two men love each other,
but the White Horses separate the combatants, and the

Director embraces White Horse 1. The Director removes his Harlequin suit, under which he wears the
costume of a ballerina or bareback rider. Tossed behind
a column, the White Harlequin Costume reappears as a
distinct entity. Then the Director removes and tosses
away the tutu, which also re-enters as a character: the
Ballerina Costume. Now wearing the leotard covered
with golden harness bells, the Director exits by the
stairway leading out of the tomb, followed by the White
Horses. Man 1 screams after his beloved Enrique a plea
to turn into a moonfish. Unheeded by the departing Director, Man 1 then "exits violently."

Man 2 and Man 3 enter from the left. The presence of Man 2 (as the woman in black pajamas with
poppies) seems to irritate Man 3, who tries to seduce
Juliet. Man 3 strips Man 2 down to his original costume
(without the beard) and pushes him offstage to the
right. The Pajamas-with-Poppies Costume now becomes a character with a smooth egglike face; "he" sits
on the steps and slowly strikes his face with his hands
until the end of the scene. Man 3 tries to be a Romeo,
but his efforts are thwarted by the Black Horse, who
puts Juliet to sleep on her tomb and, upon leaving,
promises to return the next day with some sand. Man 3
kisses the sleeping Juliet, places his ardent-expres-
sioned mask on her face, and exits on tiptoe.

Man 1 returns. He is looking for the Director, but
finds only the slumbering Juliet and the three Costumes. He embraces the Harlequin Costume and calls
it "Enrique," but the Harlequin Costume weakly protests, "I'm cold." Man 1 throws the Costume to the
ground and exits up the steps, calling more frantically
for Enrique. The nightingale's song anounces daybreak,
the fading of the dream, the closing of the theatre under the sand. The Pajamas-with-Poppies Costume continues to strike its egglike face as the curtain falls on
this scene.

One point has become clear in this sequence: identity problems exist even in the theatre under the sand. We have seen that different costumes apparently represent different facets of a personality. The proliferation of costumes calls to mind the anguished climax of Lorca's first New York poem: "Return from a Walk" (*Vuelta de paseo*):

> Coming upon my face that's different every day.
> Assassinated by heaven!
>
> *Tropezando con mi rostro distinto de cada día.*
> *Asesinado por el cielo!*[14]

That poem also contains the image of a child with the white face of an egg, a strong image of vitiated potential that mocks our usual association of the egg-symbol with fertility.

The surviving manuscript of *The Audience* includes no Scene 4, although Rafael Martínez Nadal believes that such a scene did once exist.[15] If so, it can be inferred from Scene 5 that the action covered by the missing scene must have included the public performance of *Romeo and Juliet* and the revolution that broke out during that performance, causing the Director and the horses to flee "up the hill." In 1936, Martínez Nadal saw in Lorca's possession a revised, typed draft of the play.[16] One can only hope that this later version will eventually come to light in its entirety.

Scene 5 commingles several planes of reality, some of which are suggested by its setting:

At stage center is a bed facing front and standing on end, as if painted by a primitive; in it is a Red Nude Man crowned with blue thorns. Upstage, several arches and steps leading to boxes in a large theatre. On the right, the façade of a university. A round of applause is heard when the curtain goes up.[17]

The visibility of a theatre auditorium upstage of the playing area establishes an inverted perspective: it suggests that the behavior of the theatre audience is the focus of the artist's scrutiny. The theatre box that serves as a vantage point for observing not a performance, but real-life events calls to mind an uncannily similar scenic metaphor in Jean Cocteau's 1930 surrealist film, *The Blood of a Poet (Le Sang d'un poète)*.

The Red Nude Man, whose dialogue incorporates lines from Christ's passion on the cross, questions a Male Nurse (who is perhaps inspired by the Nurse in *Romeo and Juliet*) about the tumult in the theatre, which might also evoke the street fighting in Shakespeare's play. The Nude Man is told that the revolutionaries are not interested in him, but they demand the Director's death. There is no news of Gonzalo (Man 1), who is being sought in the ruin.

Four Students wearing black academic robes enter the stage and discuss other developments; the first bomb of the revolution swept off the Professor of Rhetoric's head, but the crowd rescued his wife Elena. Perhaps Lorca was saying here that classical art, represented by Elena, had been wedded to dull and stodgy forms of expression, from which the masses instinctively wished to liberate it. Student 1 quietly notes that Elena is also Selene. This gives her an overlapping identity—that of the goddess of the moon. Since the moon is associated with death throughout Lorca's work, one may interpret this to mean that Lorca regarded classical art as fatal to the theatre, and, furthermore, that he had come to equate sexual orientation to a woman, however idealized, with death. Student 1, who expresses his fear of going outside on this moonlit night, is the same student who joyously initiates a homosexual relationship with Student 5 at the end of the scene.

The revolution began when the audience learned that Romeo and Juliet—whose real identities are quite distinct from the costumes they wear—truly love each

other, even though Juliet was played in Elizabethan
fashion by a boy actor. Student 5, leaving the theatre
boxes to join the others on stage, brings the news that
"the judge has arrived, and before they're killed they're
going to have to repeat the scene in the tomb." The students exit to watch the scene, presumably in the theatre under the sand.

The Two Thieves then assist at the death of the
Red Nude Man. The Nude Man says: "It is consum-
mated," and his upright bed spins on its axis to reveal
Man 1 lying on the reverse side of the bed, in his death
throes. The Students return to the stage. They are
shocked that the audience's response to the truth beneath the costumes was to kill both Romeo and Juliet.
The four who die almost simultaneously in Scene
5—Christ (Red Nude Man), Romeo, Juliet, and Man
1—have all sacrificed themselves for love. Their deaths
are not in vain, however, for Student 1 and Student 5
are impelled to declare their love for each other. Jubi-
lantly, they flee together through the arches while the
other students file into the university for a class in descriptive geometry. On the darkening stage, a small boy
tries to help three society women find an exit from the
theatre. His lantern illuminates the dead face of Man 1,
and the curtain falls.

The manuscript of *The Audience* includes an un-
numbered page entitled "Simple Shepherd's Solo," apparently conceived as a specialty number to be performed between scenes in front of the curtain. Martínez
Nadal's placement of this interlude between the last
two scenes of the play seems appropriate not only because all these pages were written on the same kind of
paper, but because the content of the song would have
its greatest impact at this point, and because the interlude thus serves to set the last scene apart in time and
tone from the preceding sequence of scenes. In pre-
Golden Age Spanish drama, a Simple Shepherd (*Pas-*

*tor-Bobo*), or rustic "wise fool," was often assigned to speak the prologue, because his bumbling manner would set off by contrast the slickness of the rest of the production. Although he was a comic figure, the *Pastor-Bobo* often served as a moralizer or social commentator to reinforce the didactic purpose of the play.[18] The song recited by Lorca's Simple Shepherd to his own hand-organ accompaniment is certainly moralizing in tone, however oblique its didactic import and however trivial the sound of its rinky-dink rhythm. Furthermore, one might well interpret the sequence as a kind of prologue, since the last scene of *The Audience* takes place in the same setting as the first, thus creating a circular construction.

Onstage with the Simple Shepherd is "a large cupboard full of white masks with various expressions." The song begins:

> The simple shepherd tends the masks,
> the masks
> of beggarmen and poets
> who try the patience of the vultures
> flying over stagnant waters.

> *El pastor bobo guarda las caretas,*
> *las caretas*
> *de los pordioseros y de los poetas*
> *que matan a las gipaetas*
> *cuando vuelan por las aguas quietas.*[19]

During the song the masks begin to bleat like sheep. The most logical explanation for this sequence is that the Simple Shepherd offers shallow entertainment to keep the masses happy even though he sees the hypocrisy of such "art." At the end of his song he pushes the rolling cupboard full of bleating masks into the wings, and exits.

Although the set for Scene 6 is the same as that of Scene 1 (the Director's office), some theatrical props have been added. On the floor is a large horse's head, a lifeless reminder of the Horses who do not reappear in this scene. Leaning against the wall are some cut-out scenic units: trees with clouds and a huge, staring eye. A long dialogue sequence between the Director and a Prestidigitator serves as a philosophical coda to the play. They discuss the disrupted performance, but because of their diametrically opposing views of art, they reach no agreement about its significance. The sheer artifice of the sleight-of-hand artist's work contrasts sharply with the Director's willingness to risk everything when he opened a tunnel to the theatre under the sand so that the public could face some truths about life. In contrast to the imperturbability of the Prestigitator, the Director becomes quite impatient:

Breaking down all the doors is the only way the drama has of justifying itself, of seeing through its own eyes that the rules are a wall that dissolves in the smallest drop of blood. I'm disgusted by the dying person who traces a door on the wall with his finger and goes peacefully to sleep. The true drama is a circus of arches where the air and the moon and creatures enter and exit without settling down and being lulled. Here you are trampling on a theatre where authentic dramas have been given and where a true combat occurred that cost the lives of all of its performers.[20]

Just when the Director dissolves into tears, the Servant ushers in a veiled Lady in Black accompanied by the White Harlequin Costume. She demands to know what has become of her son Gonzalo (Man 1):

Where is my son?
This morning fishermen brought me an enormous, pale, decomposed moonfish, and they screamed: Here is your son! An unceasing thread of blood trickled from the fish's mouth and all the while children were laughing and painting the soles of their boots red. When I closed my door I heard how the market people dragged it to the sea.[21]

The Director refuses to accept responsibility for Gonzalo. Offering to escort her out, the Prestidigitator covers the Lady with his magician's cape, waves his hand, and pulls away the cape: the Lady has vanished. The White Harlequin Costume is pushed offstage. The Prestidigitator calmly fans himself with a large white fan while the Director becomes progressively colder and weaker until he falls face downward on his desk. The "entire left side of the set splits apart to reveal a sky full of large clouds, vividly illuminated, and a slow scattered rain of rigid white gloves." Offstage voices repeat the play's opening lines:

"Sir."
"Yes."
"The audience is out there."
"Let them come in."

The Prestidigitator conjures a final effect: snowflakes begin to fall on stage.

Two possible interpretations of the scene come readily to mind. Martínez Nadal sees the scene as a recapitulation of problems that we now know to be without solution. This new objectivity about the preceding events of the play is possible only from the detached perspective of the afterlife, and Martínez Nadal claims that the Prestidigitator "clearly" represents Death.[22] Such an interpretation is supported by the action (the Director's demise) and by the final visual image that evokes infinity and cold. However, there is equally strong evidence to suggest that the Prestidigitator represents the kind of shallow artistry that the Director originally espoused before the Three Men in Scene 1 exposed his hypocrisy and encouraged him to open the theatre under the sand. In Scene 6 the Director argues vehemently for a theatre under the sand, but then his actions belie his words. He sells out to sleight-of-hand

trickery the moment he—like Peter denying Christ
—tells the Lady in Black that he is not the one she
should talk to about Gonzalo. That final betrayal of his
true nature signals the beginning of the cold that kills
the Director.

Much remains for literary critics and theatre artists
to discover and interpret in this amazing and complex
play. One example of Lorca's careful interrelationship
of images and structures in *The Audience* is the juxtaposition of the Roman Ruin scene and the scene in the
theatre under the sand. The former, representing the
classical mode in art, calls for a landscape of broken
arches, whereas the romantic mode exemplified by
Shakespeare's *Romeo and Juliet* elicits Juliet's image of
thousands of "empty arches"—"empty" because, being
joined at the top, they enclose a space. To Lorca, broken arches were like arms trying vainly to kiss one another.[23] If broken arches are a symbol of impossible
love, they are associated here with the restrictive form
of classical art. Within the looser structure of drama in a
romantic mode, the pillars are united at the top to form
whole arches.

Because of the many structural and thematic parallels between *The Audience* and *Play without a Title,* it
is useful to examine next that incomplete work, written
only eight months before Lorca's death. Like *The Audience,* it begins with preparations for a theatrical performance. The Author[24] comes before the curtain and addresses the spectators directly. He tells them that
"today the poet is holding you captive because he
wishes and aspires to move your hearts by showing
things you don't want to see, by shouting the simple
truths you don't want to hear." His attempt to "teach
your hearts a little lesson about reality" is based upon
his belief that the theatre, which is a lie, must be transformed into reality, which is truth. The difficulty is that
people are not moved by reality. For example, a Waiter

who brings coffee to the Author from a nearby café tells of having seen a drunken man playing a violin made of a live cat crucified on a washboard; the cat screeched as a handful of brambles was drawn like a bow across its midsection. He also recalls having seen a child and a turkey given alcohol to determine which one could better hold its liquor; after the turkey won, its throat was cut and it was eaten. Nobody had become upset over those events in real life, although theatre audiences would be horrified to see such things enacted on the stage. Despite his impassivity toward those instances of human cruelty, the Waiter is terribly frightened by the artifices of the stage and backstage, and he is capable of being moved to tears by run-of-the-mill love songs.

The Author tells a Prompter that he cannot bear to attend the rehearsal of *A Midsummer Night's Dream* because most people do not understand the play and laugh when they should not:

Everything in the work is intended to demonstrate that love of whatever kind occurs by chance and we have no power to control it. People lie asleep, the elfin Puck comes along and makes them sniff a flower, and when they wake up, they fall in love with the first person who comes along even though they may have been in love with someone else before that dream. That's how the queen of the fairies, Titania, fell in love with a peasant with the head of an ass.[25]

Just then an Actress costumed as Titania enters and declares her love for the Author, whom she addresses as Lorenzo. He spurns her love, which he believes to be as artificial as her costume, so she transforms herself onstage into Lady Macbeth. A different painted backdrop is lowered behind them and the stage lighting slowly fades to a moonlight effect. Still the Author resists her, so the Actress tries something else; she calls for blood-red lights. This lighting change coincides with the first shots of the revolution in the street outside the theatre.

The Author welcomes the revolution, hoping it will liberate the theatre from its artificiality. He calls for the doors of the theatre to be opened to outside reality while the Actress and the Prompter beg to keep them closed to preserve the theatre's mystique.

A Woodcutter with a dead-white face enters, carrying a bundle of wood on his shoulder and a small lantern in his hand. He introduces himself as Shakespeare's moon and tells the spectators that inside the theatre they are all safe from bullets, but then he sings of death:

> The air is for my October moon
> neither bird nor arrow nor sigh.
> Men will sleep. Grasses die.
> Only the silver of my ring lives on!
>
> *El aire es para mí luna de Octubre*
> *ni pájaro ni flecha ni suspiro.*
> *Los hombres dormirán. Las hierbas mueren.*
> *¡Sólo vive la plata de mi anillo!*[26]

In Shakespeare's *Midsummer Night's Dream,* the rustic portraying Moonshine in the play that is performed at Theseus and Hippolyta's wedding carries "a bush of thorns and a lantern." Perhaps this Woodcutter, like the ones in *Blood Wedding,* is a harbinger of death, but there is also an overtone of the Russian revolution in the word "October." The latter connotation is reinforced a moment later when the only one brave enough to leave the theatre to look after the children of a Woman in the audience is a Stagehand named Bakunin the Crazy. (Mikhail Bakunin was a mid-nineteenth-century Russian anarchist and longtime supporter of Karl Marx.) As soon as the Stagehand leaves, the Woman's husband, who prides himself on his gentlemanly social status and on his piety, writes down Bakunin's name in order to denounce him later. Then that orchestra-seat Audience Member takes out a pistol and shoots a Worker in the top gallery.

A group of fairies from *A Midsummer Night's Dream* carry a wounded revolutionary across the stage while the sounds of bombardment increase in volume. The Woman Audience Member has continued to scream for her children, but the Actress tells her she sounds false and demonstrates a more convincing cry of fear. The doors of the theatre are broken down, and the Author runs outside, still calling for truth on the stage of life.

Although only the first act of *Play without a Title* is extant, Lorca's intentions for Acts 2 and 3 have been recollected by several of his friends with whom he discussed the work in progress. The contemporary reality of Act 1 was to give way in Act 2 to a "twilight zone" between life and art, a morgue where the bodies of the Author and the Actress have been deposited. Pedro Suero recalled that this act, which featured a chorus of mothers, "reached true greatness" and that the work had "the force of brutal sensation and at the same time it was aflame with strange poetry."[27] Act 3 of *Play without a Title* was to be set on an exalted plane beyond danger or mundane considerations, that is, in the sky or in a heaven with Andalusian angels.[28]

In her Introduction to *Play without a Title*, Marie Laffranque points out structural parallels that exist in *The Audience*, *Play without a Title*, and *When Five Years Pass*.[29] The opening scene or act of each play sets up a realistic premise that is then intruded upon by an element of surrealistic fantasy. The middle section of each play takes place in a new and disconcerting milieu, a further departure from reality: the Roman Ruin and the theatre under the sand in *The Audience*, the morgue in *Play without a Title*, and the Sweetheart's highly stylized boudoir where a mannequin comes to life in *When Five Years Pass*. In the concluding scene or act, the setting may be the same as the first, but there is now a loftier perspective on the action, a sense of petty concerns transcended. Act 3 of *When Five*

*Years Pass* is divided into two scenes, the first in a forest clearing with a little curtained theatre stage on which is set a miniature reproduction of the library; the second in the Youth's library again.

Act 1 of *When Five Years Pass* begins with a conversation between the Youth and a bearded Old Man wearing enormous glasses, who counsels the Youth to remember in advance, that is, to remember into the future (*hacia mañana*, toward tomorrow). When the clock strikes six a Typist crosses the stage, weeping, and exits. The Youth explains that he has shut himself away from outside distractions and intends to wait patiently, even happily, for five years—until his fifteen-year-old Sweetheart returns from her travels with her Father. The Old Man seems to support that passive attitude. The Typist re-enters, still weeping over her hopeless love for the Youth; this finally provokes him to fire her. A Friend arrives and tries to liven up the Youth's outlook by joking, teasing, laughing, mixing cocktails, and bragging of his female conquests.

At the sound of thunder, the stage lights dim and turn bluish. The Youth, the Old Man, and the Friend hide behind a black screen decorated with stars. Then, hand in hand, enter a Dead Child dressed in white and a blue Cat with two red wounds. The Cat was tortured by children. The Child is frightened at the prospect of being buried in the earth. That lyrical interlude, in which the dialogue switches to poetry, ends abruptly when a hand reaches through the door and pulls first the Cat and then the Dead Child out of the room. Reappearing from behind the screen, the live characters now hold fans, blue for the Youth, black for the Old Man, and red for the Friend. They hear a woman outside disconsolately crying for her son; the Servant informs them that the portress's son died and is about to be buried, and that some children killed a cat and threw it on the roof.

A Second Friend comes to visit, surprising the others by his entrance through a second-story window; he is very young, and Lorca even suggests that the role could be played by an actress. The Second Friend tries to make the others recall a rain that carried tiny naked women inside the raindrops:

SECOND FRIEND: One year I caught one of those little rain-women and kept her two days in a fishbowl.
FIRST FRIEND: And did she grow?
SECOND FRIEND: No, she became steadily smaller, more childish, as it should be, as is right, until there was nothing left of her but a drop of water. And she sang a song.

> I return for my wings,
> let me return.
> I'd like to die becoming dawn,
> I'd like to die becoming yesterday.
>
> Yo vuelvo por mis alas,
> dejadme volver.
> Quiero morirme siendo amanecer,
> quiero morirme siendo ayer.[30]

This lovely passage might be interpreted as an erotic fantasy or as the expression of a desire to avoid death by experiencing life backward and finally returning to the womb.

The Friend and the Old Man leave. The Typist crosses the stage carrying a suitcase; she pauses in the doorway, hoping that the Youth will ask her to stay, but he merely acts sleepy. The Second Friend begins to fall asleep in a chair in a fetal position. It begins to rain, and the Second Friend sings again in his sleep the rainwoman's song. Telling the Servant to turn on the lights, the Youth asks the time. The Servant replies that it is exactly six o'clock. All the events of Act I somehow occurred within a few seconds. The act ends on a stage picture of inactivity while the song about living backward is sung again by the sleeping Friend.

In Act 2 the curly-haired Sweetheart—resplendent in a lacy, beribboned pink gown with a long train—jumps out of her ornate canopied bed to greet a Rugby Player who enters through her balcony window. He never speaks, only puffs cigars, while the Sweetheart passionately declares her love for him. He exits the way he came when the Sweetheart's Servant enters to announce the arrival of the Youth who has waited five years for her. Left alone with the Youth, the Sweetheart rejects his love and the marriage that had been arranged five years earlier. She exits, saying she will return all his gifts, even the wedding dress on the mannequin in the next room. A bluish light pervades the scene, and a Mannequin wearing a bridal gown enters. She reproaches the Youth for not having come sooner, expresses her own longing for a child, and suggests that he might be able to have a child if he can find the Typist who worked in his house and loved him.

When the Servant re-enters, the lighting returns to normal and the Mannequin's position is frozen. The Old Man makes an unexpected appearance and claims that the Youth has wounded him, but the Youth rejects him and runs off to seek the Typist. "Wait," the Father calls to the Sweetheart, who is running away with the Rugby Player. "Wait," the Old Man calls futilely after the Youth. The Mannequin remains alone, weeping.

The beginning of Act 3, Scene 1, has little apparent relationship to preceding events except for the recurring references to dream and time in the verses spoken by Harlequin, a Girl, and a Clown in front of a curtained platform in the woods. Harlequin, for example, carries two masks—one with an animated expression, the other sleeping—and says:

> Dream and time
> round the column entwine,
> the child's moan
> with the old man's broken tongue.

*Sobre la misma columna*
*abrazados sueño y tiempo,*
*cruza el gemido del niño,*
*la lengua rota del viejo.*[31]

Hunting horns sound. The Typist enters, wearing a ten-
nis dress, accompanied by a Masked Woman in vivid
yellow who recounts the romantic intrigues in her past.
The reunion of the Youth and the Typist finally occurs,
and this time the Youth knows better than to allow time
to pass between him and his love. Suddenly, the curtains of the little stage open to reveal a reduced-size
replica of the library in Act 1. The Typist goes up
the steps into the little stage setting and immediately
switches to the past tense in speaking of her love for the
Youth. An audience gathers on the platform, including
the Old Man, now dressed in blue, with visible wounds
corresponding to those of the blue Cat in Act 1. The
Dead Child crosses the little stage; both the Youth and
the Masked Woman in yellow call him "my son." Two
more masked figures enter, and the gathering is
completed with the return of Harlequin and the Clown.
The Youth asks the Typist to come with him, but she
has now become as insensitive to him as he was in Act 1
toward her. She replies: "When five years pass." While
the Youth watches from ground level, a Servant covers the Typist with a white cape and she freezes like
a statue. The Clown, Harlequin, and the Old Man all
give the disoriented Youth conflicting directions for ex-
iting from the forest.

The library setting for the last scene differs from
that of Act 1 only by the addition of the bridal-gown
mannequin, now headless and handless, and some open
suitcases. The Youth, who has just returned home, is
surprised that things are not exactly the way he remembered them: it is not clear how long he has been gone,
but he had retained a child's-eye memory of his home.
His servants' discussion of the portress's dead child

makes it apparent that the Masked Woman in yellow is
also the portress and that no time has passed since Act
1. As soon as the Youth goes off to change into his dinner suit, three card players in formal attire enter and
prepare for a card game with the Youth. They speak of
"cutting the thread," an image that associates them with
the three Fates. They see only two obstacles to their
victory over the Youth: the fact that he has a young
heart that probably deflects arrows, and the possibility
that either the Sweetheart or the Typist will return before the five years are up.

In the life-or-death game, the Youth is quickly reduced to his last card, the ace of hearts, but he delays
showing it. He tries to stall for time by offering various
liqueurs to his guests. Finally, he has no choice but to
"give up his ace," which he calls "my heart." At that
moment an illuminated ace of hearts appears on the
wall, Player 1 shoots it, and the Youth raises his hands
to his heart. Player 1 makes cutting motions in the air
with scissors, and then he and his companions exit. The
Youth's final cries for help and for love are answered
only by an echo. He dies. The Servant enters, carrying
a lighted candelabrum. The clock strikes twelve and the
play is over. If one takes the twelve chimes to be six
strokes plus their echo, then the entire play's action
occurred within a split second, that is, in the mind of
the dreamer.

This simplified recounting of the stage action in
When Five Years Pass does not adequately evoke the
play's symbolic overtones, the subtle interplay of allusions in the dialogue, and its carefully orchestrated use
of comic elements, all of which have provoked varied
and complex critical interpretations. According to
Rupert C. Allen's meticulous psychological analysis, for
example, all the characters are fragments of one central
consciousness, the inhabitant of the house of the psyche, who is undergoing a process of transformation

in attempting to discover and develop his potential.[32] Farris Anderson shows how that "quest for psychic wholeness" is metaphorically underscored by the theatrical structures in the play.[33] Dennis A. Klein focuses narrowly on the Youth's search for sexual identity and sees the Youth's encounter with other characters as fantasized heterosexual and homosexual relationships.[34] R. G. Knight believes that the Youth, immobilized by his fear of the present, relegates all his opportunities to either the past or the future, and thus the daydreamer misses out on all of life's possibilities.[35] Marcelle Auclair reports Isabel García Lorca's reading of the play as "entirely made up of my brother's childhood memories, scarcely transposed."[36]

There can be little doubt that the male visitors in Act 1 are different facets of the Youth's character: the Old Man is the cautious, self-restricting mature persona; the Friend is in an adolescent wild-oats-sowing phase of the basic personality; the Second Friend is the child that continues to exist within the man. Among the female characters there is clearly some overlapping of identity, whether or not they are also part of the central persona. The Sweetheart, the Mannequin, the Typist, and the Masked Woman in Yellow may represent an ever-changing yet ever-unattainable ideal sought by the Youth. *When Five Years Pass* is an aborted coming-of-age play. The Youth's continuing quest for love is never fulfilled. Each phase of the quest ends in a death: the Dead Child as the end of childhood innocence which can never be regained, the immobile Mannequin as the long-sustained but ultimately unfulfilling ideal of romantic love, the assassinated Youth as the irrevocable death of either the physical being or of the spirit when the will to prolong the quest is dead.

The parallel structures of Lorca's three "unperformable plays" have already been noted. Without attempting any single all-encompassing interpretation, it is worth noting other similarities in *When Five Years Pass*, *The Audience*, and *Play without a Title*. Some of the verbal or visual images that recur in two or more of the plays are: "grains of sand in the mirror," "wringing the neck of the dove," the screen, the nightingale, the masks, the Harlequin character, the theatre-within-the-theatre, the staircase that leads one lover away from the other, the balcony from which to view real life as a theatrical spectacle, the costume that becomes a character, the train of a gown trailing in the sea, and the mother weeping for a dead son. In addition, very specific non-realistic lighting changes are required in all three plays.

Lorca's claim that these three plays contained his "true subject matter" allows the conjecture that some of his lost plays in progress, as well as the plays he might have written had he lived longer, would have been—like these—experimental in form and—in a Spanish social context—controversial in content. The relatively little-known side of Lorca that is revealed in these plays puts special emphasis on role-playing and metamorphosis, lyricism curbed or juxtaposed with violent and scatological imagery, and allegorical treatment of sociopolitical concerns. In all these respects we may venture to say that Lorca's artistic direction has been subsumed and projected forward in the latter half of the century by poet-dramatist Fernando Arrabal.

# 3

~~~~~~~~~~~~~~~~~~~~~~~~~~~~~~~~~~~~~~~~

# Music and the Musicality of the Early Poetry

Lorca's earliest artistic inclination was musical. As a child he learned to play the piano and the guitar from his mother and aunt respectively. His aunt Isabel, whom he later called "the artistic directress of my childhood," taught him also to sing *flamenco* songs. His formal study of music began when he went to school in Almería, and it continued in Granada. "I was ten years old and I fell in love. . . ," he recalled in a 1918 letter to Adriano del Valle. "Then I gave myself up completely to the practice of the simple religion of Music and donned the robes of passion that She lends to those who love her. From there I entered the kingdom of Poetry where I finished anointing myself with love for all things."[1] According to Rafael Martínez Nadal, Manuel de Falla once said: "You know, everything Federico has achieved as a poet he could have equaled or bettered as a musician."[2] Among Lorca's original piano compositions were a *Poema del Albaicín* in five songs, a gypsy *zambra*, and some selections for a musical comedy.[3] Perhaps the most extensive catalogue of Lorca's musical compositions is that of Ubaldo Bardi in *García Lorca Review* (Spring 1981).[4]

Music remained Lorca's dominant interest until a year or so after the death of Don Antonio Segura Mesa, who had taught him piano, solfeggio, harmony, and composition. From about 1914 to 1918 Lorca was con-

sidered the musical prodigy of Granada, a city that supported many excellent concerts and made visiting musi-
cians the subject of much discussion and admiration.[5]

"Granada is made for music," Lorca once declared
in a lecture-at-the-piano. He described that "closed
city" as "dense with resonances, good for rhythms and
echoes, the essence of music."[6] Those same musical
resonances are characteristic of Lorca's early poetry,
which he began writing seriously around 1917. "The life
of the poet in Granada until 1917 was dedicated exclu-
sively to music," Lorca later wrote, referring to himself in the third person: "He gave several concerts and
founded the Chamber Music Society, where the quar-
tets of all the classics could be heard, in arrangements
that for certain reasons had never before been heard
in Spain."[7] One of Lorca's friends commented that "he
played Beethoven's *Moonlight Sonata* with such emotion in the *pianissimo* that it frightened me."[8]

As Lorca turned more and more to literature,
his musical orientation changed from classical to traditional. This was reinforced by his friendship with
Manuel de Falla, who—like Bartók, Stravinsky, and
other composers of classical music at that period—was
employing folk motifs in his work.[9] The 1922 Festival of
Cante Jondo that Lorca organized with Falla was only
one manifestation of his extensive study of Spanish folk
song. Lorca once told Marcelle Schveitzer that he had
collected and arranged over three hundred songs from
the region around Granada alone, and he could sing all
of them.[10] He did not limit himself to Andalusia, however, but collected folk songs from all over Spain. The
extent of his knowledge about these musical forms
is evident in the public lectures he often gave, incor-
porating musical illustrations at the piano. The major lectures, which have been published, are "Deep
Song (Primitive Andalusian Song)," "Architecture of
Deep Song," and "Lullabies."

Lorca once said: "You can put anything into music, even a doctor's prescription."[11] Music was for him as natural a means of expression as language. In any social gathering, Lorca's place was at the piano, and music was part of his conversation. José Mora Guarnido recalled that "a good dialogue with him was conceivable only in proximity to a piano, with him seated sidewise to the keyboard distractedly caressing the notes and extracting whimsical effects from them."[12] The apparent effortlessness of those musical improvisations is analogous to the deceptive simplicity of his early poetry. Lorca's talent as a composer and performer of music—like his poetic gift—sprang from a mastery of theory and technique combined with his *duende,* the dark passion that wells up unconsciously and spontaneously in certain deeply sensitive artists. The importance that Lorca placed on technique is evident in a comment he made during a rehearsal of *The Shoemaker's Prodigious Wife* with Lola Membrives's company in 1933:

You have just seen me paying attention to the rhythm and the smallest details and, in truth, one cannot proceed in any other way: songs are creatures, delicate creatures, that must be cared for so that their rhythms are not altered a bit. Each song is a marvel of equilibrium that can easily be broken: it's like a coin balanced on the point of a needle.[13]

On the other hand, the artist's technique should never be obvious to his audience. In his lecture on "Lullabies," Lorca said:

I'm trying to avoid scholarly detail that, when it doesn't have much beauty in it, wearies listeners; instead, I'm substituting emotional detail, because it's more interesting for you to know whether a melody stirs up a soft breeze that lulls one to sleep or whether a song can place a simple landscape before the just closed eyes of a child, than to know whether one melody is from the seventeenth century or whether another is written in ¾ time, all of which the poet ought to know, but not talk about, and which really is within reach of anyone who devotes himself to such subjects.[14]

As he synthesized his talents for music and poetry, Lorca professed the same principles for both arts. For example, in a piece entitled "The Rules of Music," published in the Burgos newspaper *El Diario* (August 17, 1917), he wrote that "in order to feel music, one needs a crazy, nervous imagination, and you might almost say that once the formidable dragon of technique has been conquered, [the musician] who has fantasy and passion within himself speaks unconsciously with music. . . . And the same thing happens with all the Arts and with poetry."[15] There can be no doubt that Lorca's musical sensibilities pervade his literary works. Despite the importance of his visual imagery, his poetry is for the ear. It was written to be spoken aloud, as Lorca often performed it to his own guitar or piano accompaniment. Lorca's lyricism is especially remarkable in his early poetry, that is, in all the collections up to and including *Gypsy Ballad*, which was published in 1927. (After that, having mastered the "dragon of technique," Lorca was willing to restrain his lyricism in order to find a more powerful and individual expression of his "fantasy and passion." He never totally suppressed his lyric bent, but—as we have seen in the previous chapter— experimented with more spare and jarring effects as part of an effort to grow beyond lyricism.) Thus, this chapter will examine a sampling of poems from *Book of Poems* (1921), *Deep Song* (1922), *First Songs* (1922), *Songs* (1921–1924), and *Gypsy Ballad* (1924–1927).

*Book of Poems* (*Libro de poemas*) is a collection of sixty-eight poems written between 1918 and 1920. Lorca dedicated the book to his brother Paquito (Francisco) and prefaced the poems with "Justificatory Words," explaining that "these disordered pages are a clear reflection of my heart and spirit, . . . the exact image of my days of adolescence and youth, days that link the present moment with my own recent childhood."[16] They reveal, above all, Lorca's sensitivity to nature: flowers, trees, flowing water, small living creatures of the field and woods (snails, frogs, ants, worms, crickets, butterflies, birds, and lizards). Anthropomorphism is a frequent device, as in the opening stanza of "New Songs" (*Cantos nuevos*, 1920):

> The afternoon says: "I'm thirsty for shade!"
> The moon says: "I'm thirsty for bright eyes."
> The crystalline fountain asks for lips
> and the wind sighs.
>
> *Dice la tarde: "¡Tengo sed de sombra!"*
> *Dice la luna: "Yo, sed de luceros."*
> *La fuente cristalina pide labios*
> *y suspira el viento.*[17]

All the elements of nature have the power of song in these poems. The poet, by comparison, sometimes feels that his own voice—dependent as it is upon an alphabet and words and literary allusions—is in danger of becoming hardened and losing its nightingale, as in "The Shadow of My Soul" (*La Sombra de mi alma*, 1919). In "New Songs" the poet "thirsts for new songs / free of moons and irises, and free of dead loves." After freeing himself from such literary clichés, he would sing

> A song that gets to the soul of things
> and to the soul of the winds
> and comes to rest in the happiness
> of the eternal heart.
>
> *Cantar que vaya al alma de las cosas*
> *y al alma de los vientos*
> *y que descanse al fin en la alegría*
> *del corazón eterno.*[18]

Eternity is evoked also in "Morning" (*Mañana*, 1918), whose subject is the "unending song of the water":

[Water] carries secrets          *Ella lleva secretos*
from human mouths,               *de las bocas humanas,*
for all of us kiss her           *pues todos la besemos*
and appease our thirst.          *y la sed nos apaga.*
She contains kisses              *Es un arca de besos*
from mouths now closed;          *de bocas ya cerradas,*
she is eternally hostage         *es eterna cautiva,*
and sister of the heart.         *del corazón hermana.*[19]

References in that poem to baptism and to water as an agent of spiritual cleansing are characteristic of the religious sensibility—often strongly pantheistic, but sometimes doubting—that may be glimpsed in many of the poems. Just as the snail (in "The Encounters of an Adventurous Snail," 1918) or the worms (in "Autumn Rhythm," 1920) despair of ever seeing the stars, the poet laments his inability to get in touch with God's infinity. In "The Source" (*Manantial*, 1919), the poet has prayed for deliverance from "the burning coal of sin" in his flesh by being made privy to the "secret of the water;" a distant voice then ordered him to transform himself into a tree with arms uplifted to the sky. But

I felt the deep sadness of the plant world,
its desire for wings,
for the power to throw oneself to the winds
and be carried to the white stars.
But in my roots my heart
murmured sadly to me:
"If you don't understand springwater sources,
die and lop off your branches."

*Tuve la gran tristeza vegetal,*
*el amor a las alas.*
*Para poder lanzarse con los vientos*
*a las estrellas blancas.*
*Pero mi corazón en las raíces*
*triste me murmuraba:*
*"Si no comprendes a los manantiales,*
*¡muere y troncha tus ramas!"*[20]

Satan is mentioned in several poems, which implicitly acknowledge his availability as an alternative to God. More often, however, when the poet is not striving for infinity through oneness with nature, he yearns to recover the lost purity of childhood. That is the theme of "Ballad of the Little Square" (*Balada de la placeta*, 1919), which many critics call the best work in *Book of Poems*. Its verses, as in a number of other early poems, form a dialogue in rhythms that fairly cry out for musical accompaniment. In "Ballad of the Little Square," it is a dialogue between the questing poet and some children in the square who sing about water. Thirsting, the poet feels in his mouth

| the taste of the bones | *El sabor de los huesos* |
| of my great skull. | *de mi gran calavera.*[21] |

It is as if consciousness of death were the first step in the artist's creative quest. He tells the children that he must travel very far

| beyond those mountains, | *más allá de esas sierras,* |
| beyond the seas, | *más allá de los mares,* |
| close to the stars, | *cerca de las estrellas,* |
| to beg Christ the Lord | *para pedirle a Cristo* |
| to restore to me | *Señor que me devuelva* |
| my long-ago soul of a child. | *mi alma antigua de niño.*[22] |

Although the range of themes and images is fairly limited in *Book of Poems*, there is considerable variety of form. Marcelle Auclair suggests that this collection reveals Lorca trying his wings in every poetic mode, "every rhythm, every meter—even the fourteen-foot verse line of the great Castilian lyricists, every genre, every type of *enjambement*, of caesura, every respiration, every tone, every sound. One thinks of the muted arpeggios, lightly touched, suddenly intensified, then softened again, by which a guitarist tests his instrument, takes the pulse of his listeners, warms himself up emotionally."[23]

The poems in *Deep Song* (*Poema del cante jondo,* 1921), however, all proceeded from a single, clear musical influence, that of the genuine primitive Andalusian song that Manuel de Falla and Lorca were working to preserve when they organized the 1922 Festival of Cante Jondo. Lorca's lecture on "Deep Song" acknowledges Falla's trail-blazing scholarly study of the genre and evocatively describes the melodies and poetry of the Gypsy *siguiriya* that inspired his own poetry in *Deep Song*:

The Gypsy *siguiriya* begins with a terrifying outcry, a scream that divides the landscape into two perfect hemispheres. It is the cry of dead generations, a sharp-edged elegy for bygone centuries, the passionate evocation of love under other moons and other winds. Then the melodic phrase gradually reveals the mystery of tones and sets off the jewel-like sob, a musical tear shed in the river of the voice. No Andalusian hears that cry without a shudder of emotion, nor can any regional song compare to it in poetic grandeur, and seldom, very seldom, does the human spirit succeed in shaping works of art of such naturalness.[24]

Apart from the melodies of *cante jondo,* Lorca found no other poetry to equal the purity and exactness of expression of sorrow and pain as that which "pulses in the tercets and quatrains of the *siguiriya* and its derivatives."[25]

Whereas *Book of Poems* is full of light (even at night, as in "Santiago" or in "The Interrupted Concert"), the poems in *Deep Song* echo Lorca's assertion that "deep song always sings in the night."[26] The short poem "After Passing" (*Despues de pasar*) illustrates the use of darkness as a metaphor for the sorrow that envelopes the gypsy soul:

| Children stare | *Los niños miran* |
| at a distant point. | *un punto lejano.* |
| | |
| The lamps are extinguished. | *Los candiles se apagan.* |
| Some blind girls | *Unas muchachas ciegas* |

| | |
|---|---|
| question the moon, | *preguntan a la luna,* |
| and spirals of weeping | *y por el aire asciendan* |
| ascend through the air. | *espirales de llanto.* |
| | |
| Mountains stare | *Las montañas miran* |
| at a distant point. | *un punto lejano.*[27] |

Taken as a whole, the poems in *Deep Song* describe a dry, nocturnal landscape whose characteristic silence is suddenly interrupted by the strum of a guitar or a scream of pain.

The guitar and the daggar both figure prominently in *Deep Song*. "The Guitar" (*La Guitarra*) is the third poem in the book, preceded only by two poems that establish the geographical setting for *cante jondo:* "Ballad of the Three Rivers," which contrasts Seville's Guadalquivir River with "the two rivers of Granada, / one a sob and the other blood."[28] and "Landscape" (*Paisaje*), in which "the field / of olive trees / opens and closes / like a fan."[29] The throbbing rhythms, assonances, and repetitions in "The Guitar" vividly evoke the sound of the instrument:

| | |
|---|---|
| . . . . | . . . . |
| The guitar begins | *Empieza el llanto* |
| to moan. | *de la guitarra.* |
| It's useless to calm her. | *Es inútil callarla.* |
| It's impossible | *Es imposible* |
| to calm her. | *callarla.* |
| Monotonous weeping | *Llora monótona* |
| like the water's weeping, | *como llora el agua,* |
| like the wind's weeping | *como llora el viento* |
| over the snow. | *sobre la nevada.* |
| It's impossible | *Es imposible* |
| to calm her. | *callarla.* |
| She weeps for things | *Llora por cosas* |
| far away. | *lejanas.* |
| . . . . | . . . .[30] |

Other poems in the collection that refer to the guitar are "The Six Strings" (*Las seis cuerdas*), "Malagueña,"

"Barrio in Córdoba," and "Riddle of the Guitar" (*Adivinanza de la guitarra*).

In "Memento," the poet asks

| When I die, | *Cuando yo me muera,* |
|---|---|
| bury me with my guitar | *enterradme con mi guitarra* |
| beneath the sand. | *bajo la arena.*[31] |

Four lines of that ten-line poem repeat the refrain "when I die." It is no wonder that the poet is so conscious of death, for it arrives suddenly and anonymously in the world of *Deep Song*. In "Surprise" (*Sopresa*), an unidentified body is found in the street at dawn, with a dagger in its chest. In "Malagueña," death comes and goes, goes and comes, into and out of the tavern while "black horses / and sinister people / travel the deep roads / of the guitar."[32] Near the end of the collection are two poems in dialogue with stage directions, "Scene of the Lieutenant Colonel of the Civil Guard" and "Dialogue of the Bitter One," both of which end in the death of the title character. This amalgam of music, poetry, and theatre is a noteworthy early example of Lorca's tendency to synthesize the various arts.

These brief and necessarily incomplete comments on the content of the poems in *Deep Song* cannot convey adequately their Andalusian flavor, an understanding of which requires some study of the traditional musical forms on which the work is based. An excellent book on that subject is *The Tragic Myth: Lorca and the Cante Jondo* by Edward F. Stanton, which explains the various forms of deep song and traces their influence throughout Lorca's canon.

The poems in *First Songs* (*Primeras canciones,* 1922) and *Songs* (*Canciones,* 1921–1924) are quite short, some of them only four lines, some composed entirely of lines with fewer than six syllables. This paring down of means, this understatement—along with some rather surprising metaphors—accounts for the riddle-like quality of many of the poems. They seem to challenge the reader to solve the mystery of whatever meaning lies beneath the imagery. The short poem "Clock Space" (*Claro de reloj*) from *First Songs* offers an example of the quasi-surrealistic quality of some of the imagery in these two collections:

| I sat down | *Me senté* |
|---|---|
| in a gap in time. | *en un claro de tiempo.* |
| It was a backwater | *Era un remanso* |
| of silence, | *de silencio,* |
| a white silence, | *de un blanco silencio,* |
| a daunting ring | *anillo formidable* |
| where gleaming orbs | *donde los luceros* |
| collide with the twelve | *chocaban con los doce* |
| floating black numbers. | *flotantes* |
| | *números negros.*[33] |

Time becomes a space in the silence between ticks of the clock. The numbers in a circle on a clock face lose their fixity when the poet sits down to think, for his thoughts—by their abstract nature as boundless as stars —know no temporal restrictions.

That impression of stillness in a time or space apart from the mainstream is a predominant one in *First Songs*. The book itself seems to stand apart from Lorca's other collections by its brevity: it comprises only sixteen poems, five of which—not including "Clock Space"—are grouped under the heading "Backwaters" (*Remansos*). The vagueness or lack of direction suggested by that group of poems recurs in "Captive" (*Cautiva*), which describes life as an aimless maiden who by day studies her reflection in a little mirror, but who gets lost in darkness, "weeping dew, a captive of time." In the final poem, "Song" (*Canción*), the poet asks "where is my sepulture?" and the location he is given is unclear:

In my tail, said the sun.
In my throat, said the moon.

*En mi cola, dijo el sol,*
*En mi gargantua, dijo la luna.*

Sun and moon are two dark, naked doves:

one was the other            *la una era la otra*
and both were nobody.    *y las dos eran ninguna.*[34]

Thus *First Songs* dissolves into apparent nothingness.

*Songs,* on the other hand, is an ample collection which, for the most part, seeks to affirm life through the use of positive images like daylight, flowers, and oranges. These poems are grouped under eleven different headings, the first of which—"Theories" (*Teorías*)—seems to emphasize contrasts: the difference between Saturday and Sunday in "Song of the Student" (*La Canción del colegial*), between holidays and ordinary days in "Lively Guy" (*Tío-vivo*), between night and day in "Balance" (*Balanza*), between March and April in "Refrain" (*Refrán*), between earth and sky in "Frieze" (*Friso*). One of the most subtle and intriguing juxtapositions is that in "Fable" (*Fábula*) of the unicorn and the cyclops. One possible interpretation is that the man-eating cyclops represents brute force, whereas the unicorn symbolizes man's imaginative power to create beauty. They are, in summary, "an eye / and an energy" (*una pupila / y una potencia*). Few words are needed to suggest the golden horn's "terrible efficiency" (*eficacia terrible*) in any confrontation with the single green eye. The poem ends with a warning:

Hide your targets,    *¡Oculta tus blancos,*
Nature!                        *Naturaleza!*[35]

(The Spanish capitalizes on the double meaning of *blancos:* targets and whites of eyes.) Thus do higher sensibilities hold sway over base instinct, just as art can triumph over nature.

Another section in *Songs* is headed "Songs for Children" (*Canciones para niños*). The images here—a woman crossing a Chinese bridge, a bee seeking honey in a flower, two old lizards weeping together, and others—are like illustrations from a children's picture book, and the rhythms are as simple and catchy as children's singing games, but the poetic subtext is hermetically adult. For example, in "Song of China in Europe" (*Canción China en Europa*), a young woman with a fan crosses a bridge without railings; she is looking for a husband, but the horsemen who watch her are already married to tall, pale-complexioned blondes. "The young woman / goes toward the green." (*La señorita / va por lo verde*.)[36] Carlos Feal Deibe suggests that the fan, a phallic symbol, characterizes her as an aggressive woman and that her going "toward the green" means that she follows the call of life and nature.[37] However, it seems also plausible that the woman represents China, seeking a partner in the West; she meets the West halfway on the unenclosed bridge that links the opposing cultures, but, faced with indifference, she "goes toward the green" water and probably drowns. In any case, the poetic mood established is that of explaining to a child what the figures on a willow-pattern plate or a Chinese screen are *doing*, explanations that inevitably raise more questions than they answer.

Nine poems grouped under the heading "Andaluzas" are reminiscent of the style of *Deep Song*. These include two different poems entitled "Song of the Rider" (*Canción del jinete*). The first, with the subtitle "1860," depicts a cold, black horse galloping in the black moonlight with its dead rider. Where are they going?

| | |
|---|---|
| In the black moonlight, | *En la luna negra,* |
| a scream! and the long | *¡un grito! y el cuerno* |
| horn of the bonfire. | *largo de la hoguera.*[38] |

The rider, who smells of "the flower of a knife," was probably carried back to the gypsy camp where his mother or sweetheart awaited him. The second "Rider's Song" contains the famous refrain:

Córdoba.                *Córdoba.*
Distant and lonely.     *Lejana y sola.*[39]

On his black pony, under a red moon, this rider knows that death awaits him before he reaches Cordoba.

Several sections of *Songs*, mostly in the latter half of the book, reveal a preoccupation with sexuality of an indeterminate nature. "He Died at Dawn" (*Murió al amanecer*) in "Songs of the Moon" (*Canciones de luna*) expresses the anguish of a night of longing for physical contact. A "night of four moons / and one lone tree, / with one lone shadow" is probably a night when the poet awoke four times, and although the moon changed position in the sky throughout the night, his dream was always the same, as insubstantial as a shadow.

The section "Eros with a Cane" (*Eros con bastón*) offers several portraits of women who are named in the poems: Lucía Martínez, Virginia, Carmen, Lolita, Leonarda. Virginia is the title character in the four-couplet "Spinster at Mass" (*La Soltera en misa*), which commingles a vocabulary of religiosity and suppressed sensuality. A quite different portrait is offered in "Song of the Transvestite" (*Canción del mariquita*) in the section entitled "Games" (*Juegos*); an effeminate male "adorns himself / with a shameless jasmine."[40]

Several poems in the last two sections, "Love" (*Amor*) and "Closing Songs" (*Canciones para terminar*) seem to recall specific incidences of shared love. In contrast to the playful, contented, luxuriant tone of most of those poems (which include "At the Institute and in the University," "Echo," "Idyll," and "Narcissus"), the penultimate one in the book, "Song of the Barren Orange Tree," seems to adumbrate the theme of Lorca's 1934 tragedy *Yerma*:

| | |
|---|---|
| Woodcutter. | *Leñador.* |
| Cut off my shadow. | *Córtame la sombra.* |
| Free me from the torture | *Líbrame del suplicio* |
| of seeing myself without fruit. | *de verme sin toronjas.*[41] |

This might be the voice of the artist frustrated in the process of creation, but it is equally possible that it is the lament of a man who will never have children. In either case, Lorca had allowed an unprecedented personal note to creep into *Songs,* and this may partially explain why he did not publish these 1921–1924 poems until 1927.

The artist's personal vision is fused with an Andalusian mythology in the eighteen poems written between 1924 and 1927 that comprise *Gypsy Ballad (Romancero gitano).* During those years Lorca was as much acclaimed for the spellbinding quality of his recitations as for the poems themselves, but after the 1928 publication of the poems, Spanish-speaking people everywhere became entranced by the musical rhythms and haunting themes in poems like "The Death of Antoñito el Camborio" (*Romance de la muerte de Antoñito el Camborio*) and "Sleepwalking Ballad" (*Romance sonámbulo*). Their popularity has not diminished in over fifty years; in 1978 poet-critic Manuel Durán wrote that *Gypsy Ballad* is "the most important book of poetry—the most influential, widely known, read, discussed, and learned by heart by its readers—that has appeared in Spain in the entire twentieth century to date."[42]

The *romance* (Spanish ballad) is a traditional form: eight-syllable lines, varying accentuation (or "hovering stresses"[43]), and assonance instead of full rhyme. In a 1935 lecture, Lorca said that "there are two kinds of *romances,* the lyric and the narrative. I undertook to fuse the two into one."[44] Mysterious in their deliberate understatement, yet barely restrained in their sensuality, these ballads might also be seen as symbolist dramas in miniature. With the exception of the three ballads for

three saints—"St. Michael (Granada)," "St. Rafael (Córdoba)," and "St. Gabriel (Seville)"—which are largely
descriptive, each poem contains elements of dramatic
action and characterization, as well as a deftly evoked
atmospheric setting; several contain terse exchanges of
dialogue. The result is a poetry that L. R. Lind called
Lorca's "first successful combination of music, color,
and verse."[45]

Lorca chose the designation "gypsy" for his *romancero* (collection of *romances*) "not so that it would be
specifically gypsy, but because I sing of Andalusia and
the gypsy is the purest and truest aspect of
Andalusia."[46] He wrote to Jorge Guillén in 1926 that
by using these "new themes and old suggestions" he
was trying to "harmonize the gypsy mythology with the
basic coarseness of our time, and the result is strange,
but I think that it has a new kind of beauty. I want to
succeed in making images of types that will be *understood* as such, that will be living visions of the world,
and so make the ballad *robust,* as solid as a rock."[47]

The subject of Lorca's famous "Ballad of the Spanish Civil Guard" (*Romance de la Guardia Civil Es-
pañola*), for example, is the élite police corps created by
royal decree in 1844 to keep order in isolated villages
and open countryside. Marcelle Auclair dryly notes that
this must be the world's only police system whose name
evokes a famous poem.[48] Traveling always in pairs,
wearing their blue capes and shiny, black, three-
cornered reinforced hats, the readily recognized Civil
Guard came to be feared and hated by the gypsies,
whose horse-thieving activities were sharply curtailed
by these patrols. It is the gypsies' perception of the
Civil Guard that is conveyed so robustly in lines like:

> The horses are black.
> The horseshoes black too.
> Stains of ink and wax
> glint on the capes' dark blue.

They cannot weep,
having skulls of lead.
With patent-leather souls
they travel the roads.

*Los caballos negros son.*
*Los herraduras son negras.*
*Sobre las capas relucen*
*manchas de tinta y de cera.*
*Tienen, por eso no lloran,*
*de plomo las calaveras.*
*Con el alma de charol*
*vienen por la carretera.*[49]

The hardness of the image so familiar to Andalusians is enhanced, almost ironically, by the soft musicality of the poem's rhythm and sound-values. All the nouns in the opening lines quoted above are linked by the predominance of the vowels "a" and "o," which become most emphatic in the startling *alma de charol* (patent-leather soul).

The narrative line of the poem follows the implacable progress of forty Civil Guards through the town of Jerez de la Frontera one evening when a gypsy fair is in progress. Old gypsy women clutching their jars full of coins and young girls pursued by their own long hair flee before the sabres of the horsemen, but

Rosa de los Camborios
sits moaning in her doorway
beside the platter that holds
her two severed breasts.

*Rosa la de los Camborios*
*gime sentada en su puerta*
*con sus dos pechos cortados*
*puestos en una bandeja.*[50]

The Civil Guard departs "through a tunnel of silence," leaving behind the flames of gypsy sorrow and hatred.

Several critics, most notably Gustavo Correa and

Edward F. Stanton, have written of the mythic quality of Lorca's early poetry. An Andalusian mythology is created partly by the use of characters with proper names to embody certain broad aspects of gypsy mentality. Rosa de los Camborios is one representative of the gypsy as victim, the gypsy as sufferer of that fateful affliction that Lorca describes in "Ballad of the Black Sorrow" (*Romance de la pena negra*):

> Oh, sorrow of the gypsies!
> Sorrow ever alone and pure.
> Oh, sorrow like a deep current
> and a dawn never breaking near.

> *¡Oh pena de los gitanos!*
> *Pena limpia y siempre sola.*
> *¡Oh pena de cauce oculto*
> *y madrugada remota!*[51]

The Camborio family is named also in two poems about Antonio Torres Heredia de los Camborios. The portrait that emerges in the opening lines of "The Arrest of Antoñito el Camborio on the Road to Seville" is one of male vanity and insouciance (". . . strolling slowly and gracefully. / His artfully displayed curls / glisten between his eyes."). Antonio's failure to put up a fight when five Civil Guards arrest him earns him the contempt of other gypsies: he cannot possibly be a genuine Camborio! (One is reminded of the gypsy's self-righteous assertion at the end of "The Faithless Wife": "I behaved like what I am. / Like a genuine gypsy.")

"The Death of Antoñito el Camborio" plunges immediately into violence; there are four against one, but the one goes down resisting fiercely. Who killed Antonio Torres Heredia? It was his four Heredia cousins, motivated—he thinks—by jealousy of his good looks. In the midst of the blood imagery, the tone suddenly takes a playful turn when he calls for the poet and for the protection of the Civil Guard:

Ah, Federico García,
call the Civil Guard!
Already my waist has snapped
like a broken cornstalk.
Three spurts of blood,
then he died in profile.

*¡Ay Federico García,*
*llama a la Guardia Civil!*
*Ya mi talle se ha quebrado*
*como caño de maíz,*
*Tres golpes de sangre tuvo*
*y se murió de perfil.*[52]

The appearance of an "assertive angel" to look after the
corpse adds another mythic element to the poem: the
intermingling of the human and the mysterious or divine. Angels appear also in "Brawl" (*Reyerta*):

Black angels brought
handkerchiefs and melted snow.
Angels with huge wings
of Albacete knifeblades.

*Angeles negros traían*
*pañuelos y agua de nieve,*
*Angeles con grandes alas*
*de navajas de Albacete.*[53]

Roy Campbell cautions that these are not necessarily
supernatural angels, but may be gypsy women whose
long shawls cast winglike shadows as they give succor to
the wounded.[54] It is significant, however, that in both
poems the angels minister not to the wounded, but to
the dead. With nine dead at the end of "Brawl,"

| | |
|---|---|
| Black angels were flying | *Y ángeles negros volaban* |
| in the sunset air. | *por el aire del poniente.* |
| Angels with whip-like hair | *Angeles de largas trenzas* |
| and hearts of olive oil. | *y corazones de aceite.*[55] |

The most famous poem in *Gypsy Ballad* is probably also the least translatable, and it is one of the most

difficult to analyze in terms of its narration. "Sleepwalking Ballad" opens with the oft-quoted lines:

> Green how I want you green.
> Green wind. Green branches.
>
> *Verde que te quiero verde,*
> *Verde viento. Verdes ramas.*

The first line can also mean "Green I want you to be green" or "Green how I love you green." The ambiguity and, in Spanish, the hypnotic euphony of that opening line set up an otherworldly feeling. Perhaps the characters in the poem are already dead: ghosts walking in their sleep of death, coldly reenacting the passions that once swayed them. Two men—one the father of the green-fleshed girl waiting on her balcony, one a young man whose oozing blood makes "three hundred dark roses" on his white shirtfront—provide all the movement in the poem. They exchange some dialogue in agitated rhythms that contrast with the mesmerizing descriptive sequences, and they climb together "up to the green balustrades." Suddenly all movement stops. The poem culminates in the fixed image of the green girl over the face of the cistern:

> An icicle of moonlight        *Un carámbano de luna*
> holds her above the water.    *la sostiene sobre el agua.*[56]

Did she hang herself by a rope that reflects the icy light of the moon? Or has she drowned and floated to the moonlit surface of the water?

Although all Lorca's poetry demonstrates musicality of form, in "Sleepwalking Ballad" he achieved a kind of musicality of content. The poem resonates with possibilities; it can be what its interpreter hears in it. The "story" is not meant to be followed literally, but only as a pretext for shifts of emotional coloration. A theme is established ("green skin, green hair, / with eyes of cold silver"), and then variations are played upon it ("green skin, green hair, / dreaming of the bitter sea" and "fresh face, black hair, / on that green balcony"), finally to return to the major motif. As Lorca wrote in his previously cited 1917 essay on "The Rules of Music," "whenever a work expresses a soul-state with consummate virtuosity, we can only fall silent before it."[57]

# 4

## The Visual Arts

Lorca's poems and his drawings illuminate one another. Not only do they treat the same subjects, but the characteristic features of his poetry—startling metaphors, narrative understatement, and apparent simplicity of means—are echoed in the content and style of what he called his "drawn poems" or "poems in line." Like music, drawing was for Lorca both a supplement and an alternative to verbal expression. His sketches adorned the headings and margins of the letters and postcards he wrote to friends. Even his signature was sometimes elaborated with vegetal forms, or sometimes the vertical line of the L in Lorca might be elongated as if aspiring to reach the stars, like some of the creatures in his early poetry. In one such signature, reproduced in Gregorio Prieto's *Dibujos de García Lorca,* a weeping crescent moon (with the thick eyebrows that are characteristic of Lorca's self-portraits) is sketched parallel with the top of the L; the "a" is trailed out horizontally, and beneath that line is the shadow of the crescent moon. By such simple means, the word "Lorca" is made to evoke the pull of the earth on the poet, and to suggest his dual nature: mysterious depths in counterpoint to flights of fancy.

Apart from those numerous miscellaneous drawings in margins and around inscriptions and signatures, and not counting his theatrical set and costume designs,

there are about a hundred and fifty known drawings by
Lorca.[1] Fifty-eight of those are reproduced in the 1980
edition of his *Obras completas* (*Complete Works*). Several that are not included there appear in David K.
Loughran's *Federico García Lorca: The Poetry of Limits*, and others in Prieto's *Dibujos de García Lorca*. It is
to be hoped that Lorca's set and costume designs will
be brought together and published. Despite the difficulty of establishing any certain order for the mostly
undated drawings, Patrick Fourneret categorizes them
in three major periods: before 1925; 1925–1928 (the
"Catalan period"); and during and after his stay in the
United States. The "Catalan period"—so called because
of the influence and inspiration of Catalonian art critic
Sebastian Gasch and painter Salvador Dalí, as well as
the impetus provided by the favorably received exhibit
of twenty-four of his drawings at the Dalmau Galleries
in Barcelona in 1927—was the period of Lorca's most
intense devotion to visual art, and this period shows elements of all his "styles."[2] His frequent use of colored
pencils in that period corresponds to the rich color imagery in his pre–New York poems, in contrast to the
third period's almost exclusive use of pen and ink while
his poetry became increasingly complex.

It was during the "Catalan period" that Lorca gave
his lecture entitled "Sketch of Modern Painting"
(*Sketch de la pintura moderna*, October 28, 1928),
which testifies to his sophisticated academic grasp of
twentieth-century painting.[3] His theoretical approach
to the visual arts is largely contained in the letters he
wrote to Sebastian Gasch during those years. In a surviving fragment of the 1927 letter, for example, he
wrote:

These drawings are pure poetry and pure plastic art at the
same time. I feel clean, consoled, happy, *child-like* when I do
them. And I'm horrified at having to employ a *word* to name
them. And I'm horrified by what is called *direct* painting,

which is nothing but an anguished struggle with form from which the painter *always* emerges vanquished and the work itself *dead*. In these abstractions I see *created* reality uniting with the reality that surrounds us in the same way that an actual clock unites with its concept like moss on a stone. You are right, my dear Gasch, abstraction must be united. So I should label the drawings you will receive (I'm sending them by certified mail) *Very Human Drawings*. Because almost all of them will send a little arrow to the heart.[4]

In another 1927 fragment, he wrote:

I have thought out and executed these little drawings with carefully integrated poetico-plastico or plastico-poetico criteria. And many are linear metaphors or sublimated topics, like "San Sebastian" and "peacock." I tried to choose essential features or emotion and form, or of super-reality and super-form, to make of them a *sign* that, like a magic key, leads us to *understand better* the reality that they represent in the world.[5]

The best study to date of the correspondences that exist between Lorca's poetry and his drawings is David K. Loughran's *Federico García Lorca: The Poetry of Limits,* which focuses primarily upon the choice of subject matter and on the use of line. Loughran discusses such recurrent poetic symbols and visual images as roots, hands, arrows, vines/grass/weeds, the circle, the moon, the balcony, and sailors in the drawings corresponding to the sea in the poems; and he analyzes the upward-downward tension in the poetry and drawings as proceeding from the struggle "between desire and its limitations."[6] Gregorio Prieto's *Dibujos de Federico García Lorca* is more concerned with Lorca's painterly love of color, which impelled him to apply color to his poetry even when the colors are tautologically obvious, as in "streams of white milk," "Córdoba has green olives," or "little yellow lemon."[7] Much more significant, of course, are the surprises in Lorca's poetic use of color: "black moon" (in "Song of the Rider, 1860"), "the black melons of your breasts" (in "The Spinster at

Mass"), "a hurricane of black doves" (in "Dawn"), "green wind" (in "Sleepwalking Ballad"), "a spurt of green veins" (in "The Martyrdom of St. Eulalia"), "the blue horse of my madness" (in "Your Childhood in Menton"). This list is inexhaustibly fascinating.

Prieto is not exactly accurate when he writes about Lorca's color range in terms of the frequency with which the various colors are used in the poems. Those rankings can now be checked against Alice Pollin's *Concordance to the Plays and Poems of Federico García Lorca*. Prieto posits the following order of preference of colors in Lorca's poetry: green, red (counting the word "blood" as a referent for red), and yellow, followed by black and white, gold, pink, and other more muted colors. Prieto's translators serve him badly in the English edition of his book, *García Lorca as a Painter*, when they mistakenly assert that green was "the poet's favorite color."[8] All the evidence in the poetry suggests that Lorca was emotionally repelled by green, which he associated with vegetation rooted in the earth, and thus with death. That attitude persisted even when Lorca was making a point of eliminating color from his work. For example, in his 1935 play *The House of Bernarda Alba*, the only spot of color among the women in mourning black within their whitewashed walls is Adela, who defiantly wears a green dress as if to affirm her own vitality; but she is the one character who dies at the end of the play. Throughout Lorca's poetry, the *Concordance* reveals, white is the most frequently mentioned color. In its various forms—masculine, feminine, singular, plural—the word "white" occurs a total of 150 times; it is followed by black, used 101 times; then green, used 98 times; blue, 70; pink (the word occurs 117 times, but many of these listings are for the noun "rose" or "roses," which is the same word as "pink" in Spanish); gold, 57; silver, 54; gray, 44; yellow, 39; red, 35; brown, 23. Various other color descriptions—like crimson, straw, violet—occur only once or twice. Guillermo Díaz Plaja's observation that cold colors predominate in *Gypsy Ballad* thus holds true for all of Lorca's poetry.[9]

There is clearly some color correspondence between Lorca's visual art and verbal imagery in a quantitative sense: abundant use of color in the drawings and poetry of the Catalan period as opposed to very restricted use during and after his year in America. However, the color drawings do not correspond to the poems in terms of specific color choices, nor do they even add up to a preference for cold colors. There is a much wider spectrum of colors in the drawings as a whole than there is throughout the poetry, and there is more juxtaposition of colors within most individual drawings than there is in any given poem. For example, the crayon and ink drawing at the top of the first page of a letter to Melchor Fernández Almagro uses red-orange, yellow-orange, yellow, purple, dark green, olive green, blue, pink, and brown; it shows Mariana Pineda "in her house in Granada, thinking about whether or not to embroider the flag of liberty."[10] In another of his sketches of Mariana Pineda (No. 53 in the 1980 *Obras completas*), she wears a yellow gown and clutches a red rose to her breast.[11] If any one color seems to assert itself more often than others in Lorca's colored-pencil works, it is probably yellow.

Perhaps the most striking of all of Lorca's color drawings is that of the "Virgin of the Seven Sorrows" (No. 55 in the 1980 *Obras completas*). In it the Virgin Mary, standing on a bier or what may be a Corpus Christi float, wears a head-to-foot black mantle which is open at the front to reveal her heart pierced by seven gold swords. A multicolored Andalusian background consists of a jumble of houses with red tile roofs, and yellow-green-brown hills dotted with trees and crucifixes that seem to intermingle with the white roses on the Virgin's gold halo. The area between the hills contains what appears to be an archway opening into a blue heaven. One of the hills seems to double as a close-up portrait of the Virgin, her face averted from the archway, two trees doubling as eyes brimming with tears. Gregorio Prieto recalls that he saw this drawing hanging on the wall over Lorca's bed at the *Residencia de Estudiantes* in Madrid shortly after his first meeting with the artist. Prieto admired it, whereupon Lorca took the drawing down and gave it to Prieto, pleased that he had at last met someone who saw some artistic worth in his drawings. "The Virgin of the Seven Sorrows" now hangs over Lorca's bed in the family home in Granada. Fernando Arrabal has said that seeing that drawing over Lorca's bed produced in him one of the most overwhelming emotions he ever experienced.[12] It is small wonder that Lorca is at last being taken seriously as a visual artist.

A critical review of the exhibit of Lorca's drawings in the Spanish pavilion at the 1965 New York World's Fair describes the drawings he did in Manhattan in 1929–1930 as reflections of "the nightmarish images of this verse [*The Poet in New York*] with ghostly lines that look like threads clinging to drifting phantoms."[13] That assessment evokes well the pen-and-ink drawings that make up the bulk of Lorca's work as a visual artist. Loughran sees those threadlike "ghostly lines" as roots or other vegetal forms, and this is corroborated by the number of times the words "roots" (twenty occurrences) and "branch" or "branches" (a total of fifty-four occurrences) are used in the poetry. But it is also possible to see them as veins, for the words "vein" or "veins" appear twenty-one times in the poems, and constitute an important image in the play *The Audience* as well as in Lorca's film scenario *A Trip to the Moon*. His drawing entitled "The Eye" (No. 8 in the 1980 *Obras completas*), for example, has a small, solid black almond

shape as its focal point, from which long spidery lines
float (upward like tangled seaweed), dangle (roots or
veins that stretch far to the bottom of the paper), or
meander away with a life of their own (two arrows, one
circling and finally pointing upward, the other pointing
down; and eight lines on the right side of the "eye" that
end in hands groping in various directions, several coming up against two overlapping windows, one clear, one
opaque). These separate elements recur throughout
Lorca's drawings, the blacked-in eye most notably in
the bleeding, mouthless head of the artist himself in
"Severed Heads of Federico García Lorca and Pablo
Neruda" (1934, No. 58 in the 1980 *Obras completas*).

Black drops of blood appear in several drawings:
"Severed Hands" (No. 15), "Face with Arrows" (No.
16), "Face in the Form of a Heart" (No. 17), "Slit
Throat" (No. 30), "The Lady of the Fan" (No. 32),
"Sailor" (No. 33), and "Bedroom" (No. 34), as well as
the "Severed Heads." What is most astounding about
this recurring motif is that in every case, without exception, the drops of blood are clearly falling upward; that
is, the thick, rounded, gravity-heavy end of each drop
is at the top. Perhaps they are straining to reach the
moon, which often appears at the top of the drawings as
a crescent with an open eye.

Another interesting subject that appears repeatedly in the drawings is the double face or figure, one
partially superimposed over the other. At first, the two
images are fairly clearly distinguished one from the
other, as in "The Mask that Falls" (No. 2), in which the
mask's face is shaded, its eyes closed, as opposed to the
open eyes of the clown's face; or as in "Love" (No. 23),
in which the faces of a woman and a sailor are joined
only at the lips; or as in "Legend of Jerez" (1927, No.
45), in which a shaded figure formed of dotted lines
nearly surrounds the solid outline figure he embraces.
In other drawings, the two figures often become inex-

tricably tangled up together, as in "Death" (1934, No. 25), in which one of the figures is a rather insubstantial infinity symbol made human only by the existence of a face; she appears to be pulling the skeleton right out of the upper body of the other figure, whose very corpo-real-looking legs are strolling on a patio. In the second of the drawings entitled "Figure" (No. 29), the only real clue that more than one person is represented is the two distinct sets of black-almond eyes with eyebrows. Similarly, "The Lady with the Fan" (No. 32) has two faces, overlapping torsos, and only one pair of feet, but she holds in the same hand with the fan a third face, a severed head bleeding at the neck.

Guillermo Díaz Plaja perceived two main tenden-cies in Lorca's drawing: on the one hand, a childish in-genuousness and, on the other, a surrealist quality that recalls Joan Miró, Yves Tanguy, and Max Ernst.[14] The question of Lorca's relationship to surrealism is a diffi-cult one, for he never declared any personal interest in that artistic movement, and yet its influence is unmis-takable in his more abstract drawings, in the three short plays that are usually grouped under the title *Teatro breve* ("brief theatre"), and in his 1929–1930 silent film scenario *Trip to the Moon*. Some critics have also writ-ten about surrealist elements in *Poet in New York* and in plays like *When Five Years Pass* and *The Audience*. Surrealist or not, Lorca's film scenario is the work of the visual artist more than of the writer, and it makes sense to consider his *teatro breve* in this category also, because of the cinematic inspiration and strong visual imagery that characterize those plays.

Two of the plays, *Buster Keaton's Stroll* (*El Paseo de Buster Keaton*) and *The Virgin, The Sailor, and the Student* (*La Doncella, el marinero, y el estudiante*), were published in the second issue of *Cock* (*Gallo*), the short-lived 1928 journal by which Lorca thumbed his nose at convention-bound "establishment art" in Granada. *Chimera* or *Quarrel* (*Quimera*) was written for the third issue, which was never published. *Buster Keaton's Stroll*, the most unconventional work of the *teatro breve*, is also the most reliant upon concrete visual imagery. In this play Lorca used realistic objects, landscapes, and characters in unexpected contexts and relationships in order to illuminate—as Lorca's lecture "Imagination, Inspiration, and Evasion" of that same year suggests—the infinite possibilities of "the invisible reality in which man moves."[15] This procedure seems very close to surrealism, and, indeed, many critics have found parallels between certain plays and poetry by Lorca in this period and the famous 1929 film *An Andalusian Dog* (*Un Chien andalou*) by Luís Buñuel and Salvador Dalí, although Buñuel himself felt that Lorca's work was too intellectually conceived to be claimed by the surrealists.[16]

*Buster Keaton's Stroll* seems to have been conceived in the silent film mode, with dialogue so minimal that it could easily be incorporated on title cards. In a letter to Guillermo de Torre, Lorca actually referred to the play as "photographed dialogue."[17] Moreover, the only mention of color in the three-page play is the "gray butterflies" that are chased by a riderless bicycle. Lorca must have envisioned the work in black and white, like the many American silent-film comedies he had seen at the Cine Club in the *Residencia de Estudiantes*.

The play opens with the cock-a-doodle-doo of a Rooster, played by an actor. Buster Keaton enters with his four children, kills them with a wooden sword, counts the corpses, and rides off on a bicycle. He passes a Black Man standing amidst some old rubber tires and gasoline cans, eating his straw hat, but Buster Keaton remarks only that it's a beautiful afternoon for a bicycle ride. A parrot "circles in the neutral sky." Almost before the incongruity of that bird's presence can sink in,

an Owl enters and sings "Chirri, chirri, chirri, chi." The
proximity in time of appearances by the Rooster that
crows to announce daybreak and the Owl that flies by
night suggests a cinematic collapse of time like that in
Act 1 of *When Five Years Pass,* or a surrealistic juxtaposition of day and night.

It is difficult to conceive of a stage production of
*Buster Keaton's Stroll* that would not employ a narrator
to read the stage directions, for besides indicating necessary action and visual effects, the stage directions
have a poetic vitality of their own; taken together they
form a prose-poetry sequence that is dense with bizarre
images. Following his encounter with the Owl, for example:

> Buster ineffably cuts through bulrushes and a field of rye. The
> landscape is narrowed down between the wheels of the bike.
> The bicycle has only one dimension. It can enter books and
> stretch out in the bread oven. Buster Keaton's bicycle does
> not have a saddle of caramel or pedals of sugar, as bad guys
> might wish. It's a bicycle like others, except that it's the only
> one wrapped up in innocence. Adam and Eve would run away
> in fright if they saw a glass full of water, but, on the other
> hand, they would embrace Buster Keaton's bicycle.[18]

Rupert C. Allen suggests that in referring to a "caramel
saddle" and "sugar pedals" Lorca was thinking of the
trick bikes used in Mack Sennett comedies: they often
had sticky seats and pedals that crumbled away under
the rider's feet.[19]

Buster Keaton sighs of love and falls off his bicycle,
which rolls away crazily, half a millimeter above the
ground in pursuit of two large gray butterflies. This is
obviously an overlapping of two standard movie cartoon
devices used in the 1920s, the animated machine and
"seeing stars" or butterflies after taking a fall. Picking
himself up, Buster Keaton says: "I don't want to say
anything. What am I going to say?" A Voice calls him
"Fool." Buster Keaton continues on foot. There is a po-

etic description of his eyes and a provocative reference
to the inhabitants of the city of Philadelphia, which glit-
ters in the background.

Then he is greeted by an American Woman. According to the stage directions, "Buster Keaton smiles
and takes a close-up look at the woman's shoes. Oh,
what shoes! We cannot allow such shoes. It must have
taken three crocodile skins to make them." Critical interpretations of that stage direction are emblematic of
various overall approaches to the play. Rupert C. Allen
sees the "three crocodile skins" as a reference to the exaggerated size of the shoes: the American Woman is
wearing the clown shoes of slapstick comedy.[20] Barbara
N. Davis takes this to be an implicit criticism of American indifference to slaughter.[21] Both Allen's contention
that the play is a film critic's commentary on the declin-
ing art of film comedy and Davis's view of it as social
criticism focusing on American neglect of human values
are elaborated in their meticulous analyses of the work.
Virginia Higginbotham calls *Buster Keaton's Stroll*
"a modern farce,"[22] and Robert G. Havard sees it as
"an essentially lyrical expression which only utilizes or
feeds on the cinema."[23] That all these interpretations
are valid is a tribute to the artistic magnitude of this
brief piece.

The American Woman asks Buster Keaton for a
sword decorated with myrtle leaves and a ring with a
poisoned stone; both objects may connote either eroticism or romanticism. The scene itself suddenly becomes quite romantic—"Hollywood lyricism," Allen
calls it—when four seraphim with sheer gauze wings
dance among the flowers. A distant piano waltz is heard
in the moonlight. "Autumn has invaded the garden, just
like water into a geometrical sugar lump." Buster Keaton sighs that he would like to be a swan, but where
would he put his hat, his wing collar, and his moiré
necktie? A Young Woman in 1890s dress, with the head

of a nightingale, bicycles up to him and asks his name. When he introduces himself as Buster Keaton, she falls from her bicycle in a faint and "her striped-stockinged legs tremble on the lawn like two dying zebras." In a thousand different performances all given at the same time, a gramophone has announced: "In America there are nightingales." Buster Keaton kneels beside the Young Lady and, addressing her as Señorita Eleonora, begs her forgiveness. Allen suggests that the Young Lady represents the great actress Eleonora Duse and, by extension, the demise of the legitimate stage brought about by the film industry.[24] The play ends with the image of gleaming stars of police badges on the Philadelphia horizon. This final visual effect may be intended as an evocation of American authority as Allen suggests, or Lorca may have been thinking of the Keystone Kops who were always ready to give chase to the unfortunate clown.

It is not entirely likely that Lorca intended *Buster Keaton's Stroll* as social criticism, since his impressions of the United States were rather vague before the 1929 visit that developed his social conscience far more fully than before. Apart from its intrinsic interest as a piece of experimental literature or as a film scenario or as a viable work for the stage, *Buster Keaton's Stroll* marks an important step in Lorca's progress toward the synthesis of all the arts that he was to achieve in his last plays. It may have been "only an exercise," as Virginia Higginbotham notes, "but it represents the development of Lorca's conception of theatre as visual spectacle rather than witty repartee."[25]

*The Virgin, the Sailor, and the Student* is unconventional in less striking ways, since most of its visual imagery occurs in the dialogue. An Old Woman hawking snails in the street catches the attention of the Virgin on her balcony, who remarks that the snails piled up in the basket look like an ancient Chinese city. The

Old Woman's remarks about her snails seem to release the Virgin's Freudian inhibitions: the girl volunteers that she is embroidering all the letters of the alphabet on her linens so that a man may call her by whatever name he likes. There may be implicit social criticism in the pointed contrast between the Old Woman in rags who scurries away huddled close to the wall and the Virgin whose hands are "pale from the insomnia of silk and embroidery cloth," and perhaps the play is an early example of Lorca's concern for the plight of Spanish women as victims of excessive social constraints.

The fact that the Virgin sings of a Sailor and a Student before either of them appears suggests that the remainder of the play after the Old Woman's exit is the Virgin's erotic fantasy. Suddenly the view from the balcony includes a bay with a flag-bedecked motorboat. A Sailor enters and flirts suggestively with the Virgin, mentioning her thighs and his own nude physique, but abruptly breaks off and is last seen playing an "accordion as dusty and tired as a seventeenth century." The Student, upon entering, declares that the century is going too fast and that he is fleeing from the year ahead. He asks for water and offers to climb up and spend the night with the Virgin, but she thinks of her mother and hesitates. He apparently dies of thirst, while she contemplates jumping off the letter Z into the abyss.

The last work of the *Teatro breve* is the posthumously published *Chimera* (or *Quarrel*, since *Quimera* has a double meaning in Spanish). Set in front of a family home, it is the haunting study of a man's departure from his wife and children for a long trip. Enrique pauses on the doorstep as his six children call out from inside the house their requests for the gifts he will bring on his return. An Old Man, hoping to earn a tip by carrying the suitcases, claims that he used to be the coachman for the family of Enrique's Wife. His insistent memories begin to irritate Enrique, who fears he will miss his train. The Old Man draws a comparison between trains, which are silly and don't scare anyone, and horses, which are a force to be reckoned with, although Enrique's Wife was never afraid of horses. The sexual connotations are obvious.

The children call out to their father again; they have changed their minds about what gifts they want. They are heard quarreling among themselves until Enrique harshly quiets them and says that they will all be satisfied. Enrique and the Old Man leave. The Wife appears in the window and undresses herself as she watches her husband get smaller and smaller, so small that she could swallow him as if he were a button. One of the children, a Little Girl, changes her mind again and now cries for the first thing she had asked her father to bring. Her sobs end the play.

The simplicity of the action in *Chimera*—a loving farewell marred by mounting anxieties and a quarrel—creates a sense of foreboding by understatement. As the sole elements of the setting, the door and the window take on tremendous significance. Although superficially realistic, the play has an eerie quality similar to that of a Chirico painting. In a literary sense, *Chimera* would be closer to the one-act plays of the symbolist Maeterlinck than to any expressionist play. The absence from the stage of the six children, who (except for the Little Girl at the end) are heard but not seen, is a visual equivalent of Maeterlinck's silences. Although Maeterlinck's influence is apparent also in Lorca's early play *The Butterfly's Evil Spell*, *Chimera* is unique among Lorca's plays in its concomitant normalcy and bleakness of atmosphere. It is unique also, as Barbara N. Davis notes, in that it is Lorca's only play with a complete family: father, mother, and children.[26] It furthers the notion that in 1928 Lorca's artistic direction was still open to change. The direction that he subsequently took was determined in large part by his 1929–1930 visit to the United States.

The "unperformable" plays that Lorca wrote after

his stay in America have been discussed in chapter 2, and the difficult poems collected in *Poet in New York* will be examined in chapter 6. A less known product of that watershed year in Lorca's creative development is his silent film scenario *Trip to the Moon* (*Viaje a la luna*), which can be fruitfully compared with those plays and with the New York poems (see, for example, my article "Lorca in Metamorphosis: His Posthumous Plays," *Theatre Journal,* March 1983). It also contains some of the images and preoccupations of earlier drawings, poems, and plays: isolated parts of bodies, an eye superimposed upon a fish, black ink drops on a white expanse, a moon that emerges from a skull, veins, a guitar whose strings are cut by a hand with scissors, trees swaying in the wind. *Buster Keaton's Stroll* is recalled in shots 3 and 9 of *Trip to the Moon*: "Big feet run rapidly, wearing exaggerated long stockings of black and white" and "two legs oscillate rapidly." The couple that switches without apparent motive from a sensual kiss to eye-gouging violence in shots 63 through 67 may be compared to the abrupt changes that occur in the Virgin's flirtation with the Sailor and the Student. Less direct is the comparison with *Chimera* evoked by the film scenario's shots of doors closing, women weeping, and trains rushing.

Although Lorca's poetry abounds with violence and eroticism, nowhere does he offer violence and eroticism in such a clinical, brutal, and even repulsive manner as in *Trip to the Moon*. Hastily written in two days, its very spontaneity makes it a good index to Lorca's emotional state at the time. It mingles Spanish motifs (shot 41, for example, features Roelejunda, a spooky woman of Spanish gypsy legend, who constantly weeps tears of blood) with jarring images of New York, where Lorca's sense of cultural alienation was much magnified by his inability to speak or understand English. That feeling of isolation caused him to seek out Spanish-speaking

people, one of whom was Emilio Amero, a Mexican
graphic artist who was then doing commercial designs
in New York. Amero screened for Lorca a film he
had made about shop machines in motion. The two
discussed Buñuel and Dalí's surrealist film *An Andalusian Dog*, and Lorca then wrote his scenario, which
he left with Amero.[27] *Trip to the Moon* has, to date,
been published only in an English translation (in
volume 18 of *New Directions in Prose and Poetry*,
1964).[28] The Spanish original is still in Amero's possession, but it has apparently been authenticated by Lorca's brother Francisco.[29]

The 78 shots that comprise *Trip to the Moon* include such standard cinematographic devices as fades,
superimpositions, animation (as when the letters HELP!
HELP! fall out a window), and a kaleidoscopic lens effect.
There are several on-screen metamorphoses, but none
of them necessarily requires a stop-action technique.
J. F. Aranda envisions the film that would result from
Lorca's scenario as replete with "shallow fields of strong
surrealist plasticity."[30] There is no narrative continuity,
but certain images and characters reappear several
times. The script begins with a shot of an empty bed.
The bed is seen again near the end (shots 74–75) with a
corpse lying on it. The corpse is that of a man with
veins painted on his face and body, who appears in several earlier shots. Thus the premise of the film might be
to chronicle the rush of images in the man's mind and
bodily sensations experienced at the moment of his
death; that is, during his "trip to the moon." There are
abused children, fish palpitating in agony, women
mourning, various people vomiting, and close-ups of
both male and female sexual parts.

In shot 56, "a head looks stupidly about, approaches the screen, and fades into a frog; the man with
the veins squeezes the frog between his fingers." Human cruelty to animals as well as to children occurs sev-

eral times in the scenario, and the frog also appears in shot 35 in juxtaposition to a human head. If there is a subtextual meaning to be found in this, it may be that the dying man literally feels as though his head is being squeezed and mentally relates it to his own misdirected lust, of which the frog is a standard symbol. Certainly, frustrated love is the predominant concern that surfaces from the bizarre collage of images. The object of the man's desire is a boy in a harlequin suit, who is seen in shot 54 with a nearly nude woman in an elegant cocktail bar where people are so drained of vitality that they cannot raise their wine glasses to their lips. The appearance of the man with veins, "gesturing and making desperate signs and movements that express life," amazes the men in the bar, all of whom vomit in shot 60. A few shots later the boy in the harlequin suit, frustrated by the nude woman, takes off his jacket and wig and becomes the man with veins. In shot 69, the girl "fades into a plaster bust and the man with the veins kisses her passionately." That contact with a lifeless object may be intended to suggest that he is going through the motions of being heterosexual. It may also be what kills him, for the names "Elena, Helena" appear on the screen and fade into violent screams. As mentioned in chapter 2, the character named Elena or Helena (or Selene, the goddess of the moon) in *The Audience* is associated with death.

If this interpretation is correct—that shots 1 through 73 represent a dying man's last conscious thoughts and sensations—then shots 74 through 78 stand outside the man's consciousness:

75  A fellow in a white dressing gown and rubber gloves, and a girl dressed in black come in. They paint a mustache on the dead man's head and kiss each other amid great bursts of laughter.

76  A cemetery bursts from them and they are seen kissing over a tomb.

77  View of a cinematic kiss with a background of other persons.
78  And finally . . . landscape of the moon with trees swaying in the wind.[31]

The painting of a mustache on a dead man's face might be seen as a surrealist's aesthetic gesture, like painting a mustache on the Mona Lisa, but it probably also has something to do with Lorca's preoccupation with sexual identity and his awareness that after death the artist's nature will be defined by superficial clues in the work he leaves behind, by people who do not at all understand his true nature. The poetic equation of the moon with death, suggested by the imagery of shots 18 and 49, is brought to completion in the final shot of the trip's destination.

At least two critics believe that *Trip to the Moon* was intended as homage to Luís Buñuel.[32] Despite the obvious influence of Buñuel and the possible influence of Cocteau (the rubber gloves in the death scene), *Trip to the Moon* is a very personal and original work. According to Amero, Lorca also made sketches to show how some of the shots ought to be handled.[33] There can be no doubt that Lorca's well-developed skills as a visual artist—as a painter, sketch artist, designer of sets and costumes, and potential filmmaker—merit far more critical attention than they have received.

# 5

~•~•~•~•~•~•~•~•~•~•~•~•~•~•~•~•~•~•~•~•~

# Folk Entertainments

Lorca's artistry matured steadily in the last decade of his life. He extended his musical research back to the medieval and Renaissance periods, with attention to other regions as well as Granada.[1] As noted in chapter 4, his drawings became less grounded in reality as his poetry made increasingly sophisticated use of metaphor. As a dramatist he gradually developed the skills that would enable him to write the three tragedies and one bittersweet comedy about the plight of Spanish womanhood that are considered to be his masterpieces. Throughout these processes of maturation and refinement, however, he paused repeatedly to refresh himself, as it were, at the wellspring of simplicity and naïveté: his Spanish folk heritage.

In *The Comic Spirit of Federico García Lorca*, Virginia Higginbotham discusses the continuation in Lorca's farces of Spanish theatrical traditions dating as far back as the fifteenth century. *The Shoemaker's Prodigious Wife* (*La Zapatera prodigiosa*), she claims, "is composed almost entirely of techniques borrowed from the early *entremeses*."[2] (The *entremés*, a farcical form perfected in the seventeenth century by Miguel de Cervantes, combined slapstick humor with serious insight about human frailties.) According to Marie Laffranque, Lorca wanted to revive the form of the medieval mystery play, which mingled biblical content with

realistic and humorous material from everyday life, as a
vehicle for content that would be responsive to the concerns of contemporary audiences.[3] This idea has been
propounded also by two other major twentieth-century
dramatists. In 1918 Vladimir Mayakovsky completed
*Mystery Bouffe,* in which elements of the mystery
play—including a low-comedy version of Hell—are
used to illustrate the rise to power of the Russian prole-
tariat. Italian playwright-director Dario Fo gave the
same title, *Mistero Buffo* (1969), to his play utilizing the
loose structure and popular entertainment devices of
the mystery play; his purpose was to reach rural and
working-class audiences by starting from what they
know and can appreciate. Lorca proceeded in much the
same way not only in the historical drama, puppet
plays, and farces that he wrote, but also in the works by
earlier Spanish authors that he prepared for presentation by *La Barraca,* the touring theatre group he
founded in 1932. He was profoundly sincere when he
said in his "Talk about the Theatre" (February 2, 1935)
that "the theatre must catch the social and historical
pulse, the drama of the people and the genuine color of
their landscape and spirit, with laughter or with tears;
unless it does that, the theatre has no right to proclaim
itself as theatre."[4]

Lorca's *Mariana Pineda* belongs in this tradition,
because the title character is based upon a historical figure who had already become a part of Granada's folk
heritage when Lorca wrote his play in 1925 (it was produced in 1927). Folk ballads, paintings, and stories, as
well as a marble statue in a square named after her,
commemorate the heroic woman who stitched a banner
of liberty for those who sought to overthrow the des-
potic Ferdinand VII; she was executed in 1831, refusing
to name the conspirators. Lorca did not envision an
epic drama; he "was moved by the simple, lyrical, and
popular conception of Mariana."[5] He added an appro-

priately romantic dimension to history by characterizing Mariana primarily as a woman in love. It is only when she realizes that the republican leader she loves so deeply places his devotion to liberty ahead of her that Mariana's own political consciousness is aroused, and she goes willingly to her death, resolved that her name will be fused with the ideal of liberty.

In order to "catch the social and historical pulse" and the "genuine color of the landscape and spirit" of the people of Granada, Lorca opened *Mariana Pineda* with a prologue set before a backdrop painted to look like an old engraving of the now-demolished Moorish arch of the Cucharas and a view of the Plaza Bibarrambla in Granada. Voices of children are heard, singing a popular ballad about Mariana Pineda, a song well known in Granada. The main action of the play, too, is interspersed with songs as well as a recital of the ballad of the Duke of Lucena, which is emblematic of Mariana's story. The poetic verse dialogue carries the shifting moods of the play through moments of gaiety, lyricism, passion, suspense, and even humor. Most evocative for Granadans are the frequent references to specific local place names: streets, churches, public buildings, and the river Genil. When Mariana hopes to be rescued, she is reminded that "Andalusians talk a lot, but when it comes to action . . ." That local flavor is subsumed into a larger spirit of patriotism when Mariana defies Pedrosa, the dishonorable representative of the king: "This cannot be! You cowards! Who orders such atrocities in Spain?" Later she says: "Liberty! I offer myself completely so that your brilliant spark will never be snuffed out." At the end, as she is led off to be beheaded (a fate that is subtly adumbrated by several references throughout the play to her pretty white neck), Mariana Pineda invokes both liberty and love, while the chorus of children reprise the folk ballad, and the evening bells toll.

Although some folk elements are evident in every play Lorca wrote, his puppet plays remain closest of all to their popular sources. The title character of his two extant puppet plays, *The Tragicomedy of Don Cristóbal and Miss Rosita* (or *The Cachiporra Puppets,* 1928) and *The Puppet Theatre of Don Cristóbal* (1931), is the major stock character of Spanish traveling puppet theatres, much like the English puppet stage's Punch. Don Cristóbal is a greedy, lascivious, quarrelsome old man who frequently flies into violent rages and beats up or kills other puppets with his ever-present billy club. The Cachiporra troupes, which occasionally performed in Valderrubio when Lorca lived there as a child, were Lorca's earliest theatrical influence, and that influence never left him. Several critics suggest that his major plays profited directly from techniques he mastered in his puppet plays: broad strokes of character delineation, violent action, and dialogue that mingles fancifulness with earthy popular expression. Certainly the puppet shows have much in common thematically as well as technically with his more ambitious farces, *The Shoemaker's Prodigious Wife* (1926, revised 1935) and *The Love of Don Perlimplín with Belisa in the Garden* (1928).

In traditional Spanish puppet performances, Don Cristóbal often engaged in impromptu dialogue with audience members, and this apparently was a feature of the lost puppet play *The Girl Who Waters the Basil and the Inquisitive Prince* that Lorca wrote for performance at the 1923 Twelfth Night entertainment he organized with Manuel de Falla for local children in Granada. The two extant puppet plays, as well as *The Shoemaker's Prodigious Wife,* employ direct address to the audience in their prologues. Not only is that device used also at the beginning of the posthumous *Play without a Title,* but the points made in the prologues of those plays about the nature of theatrical art in Spain are similar to the preoccupations that emerge in *The Audience*, the other posthumous play, which serves as a key to much of Lorca's thought (see the discussion of it in chapter 2). In announcing *The Tragicomedy of Don Cristóbal and Miss Rosita*, for example, Mosquito says: "My company and I have just come from the bourgeois theatre, the theatre of counts and marquises, a theatre of gold and crystal, where gentlemen go to fall asleep and the ladies . . . to fall asleep as well. My company and I felt stifled there." But once they caught a glimpse of the real world in all its fresh beauty, Mosquito and his friends ran away "to the countryside, looking for ordinary people, to show them things, the littlest things, the littlest tiniest things in the world, under the green moon of the mountains, under the rose-colored moon of the seashore."[6] When the play was performed in Buenos Aires in March 1934, the prologue was prefaced by a "Dialogue between the Poet and Don Cristóbal." Don Cristóbal spoke of his long association with Lorca and of his doubts about performing that night in a boulevard theatre with painted backdrops and an artificial moon, because he was used to performing in the Andalusian countryside for shepherd boys and for girls who blush easily. Lorca replied that Don Cristóbal was a mainstay and a progenitor of all theatre, that even Shakespeare's Falstaff was his descendant, and that even though he had been so long neglected, the theatre would eventually return to its origins through him. Lorca added: "I've loved you since I was a child, Cristobita, and when I become an old man I'll get together with you again to entertain children who have never been to the theatre."[7]

The prologue to *The Puppet Theatre of Don Cristóbal* prepares its audience for the bawdy language they will hear in the dialogue, which the Poet "picked up from popular speech." The audience is told that "all traditional puppet shows have such rhythms, such fantasy,

and such enchanting spontaneity as the poet has pre-
served in the dialogue. The puppet show is the expression of folk fantasy, and illustrates its mood of grace and
innocence. So, then, the poet knows that the audience
will hear joyfully and placidly the expressions and
words that are born from the earth and that will serve
as a cleansing force in a time when bad intentions, errors, and confused values make their way even into the
closest family circle."[8] The Poet then tries to tell his listeners that he would like also to expand their horizons;
for instance, he might even show that Don Cristóbal
has some basic goodness in him. But the Director cuts
off the Poet, reminding him that he gets paid for giving
the theatre what it expects from him. Because of his
economic dependence, the Poet is not free to invent
new approaches. Later in the play, the Poet sneaks out
to address the audience once more. He suggests some
creative possibilities for the play, given the puppet
characters that he has to work with, "but the theatre
owner keeps the characters confined in a little iron box,
so that the only ones allowed to see them are ladies
with silken bosoms and silly noses and gentlemen with
beards who go to clubs and say 'Ca-ram-ba.'"[9]

The premise of the two puppet plays is the same as
that of the two farces: an old man risks losing his honor
when he marries a young girl, since she will be attracted to younger men. In both puppet plays, Don
Cristóbal purchases the hand of Rosita from her parent.
In *The Tragicomedy of Don Cristóbal*, Rosita is in love
with the poor but good-hearted Cocoliche, and she is
also pursued by a fickle former suitor, Currito. Cocoliche and Currito both hide in armoires in Rosita's
house. After her wedding to Don Cristóbal, they
scream every time he kisses her. When he discovers
them, Don Cristóbal is stabbed by Currito. There is a
hysterical chase sequence, and then—his gear strip-
ping noisily—Don Cristóbal falls dead. Cocoliche no-

tices that there is no blood: Don Cristóbal was not a real person!

In *The Puppet Theatre of Don Cristóbal*, the nasty old Cristóbal with his billy club kills a sick man and steals his victim's money in order to marry Rosita. Rosita is willing to be sold in marriage to no matter whom, because she has plenty of lovers. She says:

> I'd like to be
> on the divan
> with Dan,
> on the mattress
> with Chris,
> on the daybed
> with Ed,
> in the armchair
> with Blair,
> on the floor
> with the one I adore,
> against the wall
> with the handsome Paul,
> and on the chaise longue
> with Dan, with Ed, with Blair,
> with Paul and with Chris.
> Ay! yi! yi! yi!
>
> *pero yo quisiera estar:*
> *en le diván*
> *con Juan,*
> *en el colchón*
> *con Ramón,*
> *en el canapé*
> *con José.*
> *en la silla*
> *con Medinilla,*
> *en el suelo*
> *con él que yo quiero,*
> *pegada al muro*
> *con el lindo Arturo,*
> *y en la gran "chaise-longue"*
> *con Juan, con José, con Medinilla,*

*con Arturo y con Ramón.*
*¡Ay! ¡ay! ¡ay! ¡ay!*[10]

She would even be willing to marry an animal, because "after all, there's really not much difference." After their wedding, Don Cristóbal falls asleep. Rosita begins to receive visits from her lovers; each time the sound of her kisses awakens Don Cristóbal she soothes him back to sleep. Finally, she runs off stage to give birth to four babies. On hearing the news, Don Cristóbal beats Rosita's Mother with his club despite her insistence that he is the father. He would probably kill the Mother, but the Director enters just in time and ends the show with another speech to the audience.

Like Japanese plays that are written to be performed interchangeably by Kabuki actors or Bunraku puppets, Lorca's puppet plays might well be staged as live theatre, although some stylization seems inevitable: puppetlike movements and gestures, choreographed violence, nonrealistic settings, including the "little frame" (*retablillo*) around the setting so that characters can flop forward across the "footlights" when they die. Although the farces are written for live actors, they are quite similar to the puppet plays in certain stylistic details. In *The Love of Don Perlimplín with Belisa in the Garden*, "a flock of black paper birds flies past the balcony." When Don Perlimplín bargains with Belisa's Mother for a marriage contract, she tells him that Belisa is "a lily. You see her face? Well, you should see the rest of her! Like sugar. But, excuse me. It's not necessary to mention such things to a person as modern and knowing as you."[11] Such erotic innuendo recalls similar dialogue in the arrangements made between Don Cristóbal and Rosita's Mother in *The Puppet Theatre of Don Cristóbal*: "She has two little breasts like two little oranges and a bottom like a little cheese."[12] A fanciful sequence in *The Shoemaker's Prodigious Wife* involves a butterfly

fluttering about the room, an effect that is best
achieved by a paper butterfly on a puppet wire. Among
the characters in that farce is Don Mirlo (Don Blackbird), who wears a black dress suit with short trousers
and "moves his head like a wire doll," a characterization
effected by much the same means as that of the insect-
like Mosquito in *The Tragicomedy of Don Cristóbal*.

   *The Love of Don Perlimplín with Belisa in the Gar-
den* is the story of the awakening to love of a fifty-year-
old man who was always satisfied with his books and
was innocent of women until his elderly servant Marcolfa persuades him to court and marry the young girl
next door. He falls in love with his bride on their wedding night when he peeps through the keyhole as she
dresses, and he becomes obsessed with her lovely
body. As soon as Perlimplín and Belisa go to bed and
turn out the lights, two *duendes*—elfin spirits played
by children—draw a curtain across the scene, "because
it's best to cover up the shortcomings of others." When
the curtain opens, it is morning. Don Perlimplín sits up
in bed; on his head are the large gilded antlers of a stag,
the horns of a cuckold. All five of the room's balconies
are open, each with a ladder propped up to it and a hat
on the ground below. Don Perlimplín kisses Belisa and
realizes that she has been kissed by someone else. She
falls asleep exhausted, while he experiences for the first
time the pain of unrequited love.

   Marcolfa is appalled that her master was cuckolded
by five men on his wedding night, but Perlimplín's love
for Belisa has already progressed to a higher plane.
When he tells Marcolfa that he is happy because he
has "learned many things, and above all can imagine
things," he means that he has learned to love and he
can now imagine the bliss of mutual love. He seems to
get vicarious gratification from the mutual love that now
seems to exist between Belisa and a mysterious young
man in a red cape who flits through the garden, tossing

her letters that rhapsodize not about her soul, but about her "white, soft, trembling body." Belisa confesses to Perlimplin that she has never seen this man face to face, but she loves him with all her being.

The final scene is set in the moonlit garden where Belisa is to meet her mysterious lover. Perlimplin has arranged the singing of a lushly sensuous serenade for Belisa's entrance. He tells her that he is going to kill the man she loves so that he will be hers completely and never leave her. Perlimplin embraces Belisa and exits. Then a figure wrapped from head to foot in a red cape enters, staggering as if wounded. He says that Belisa's husband stabbed him, shouting, "Belisa has a soul now!" Belisa sees that the man in the red cape is Perlimplin himself. He says: "Do you understand? I am my soul and you are your body." Belisa does not seem to understand that the young man she loves was noncorporeal, a creation of the imagination. She continues to ask after the young man as Don Perlimplin dies. Only the aged Marcolfa understands the full extent of Perlimplin's sacrifice.

Although the ending is tragic in tone, *The Love of Don Perlimplin with Belisa in the Garden* is basically a farce, because the one-dimensional characters—the deceived old man, the know-it-all servant, the bewitching child-woman, the social-climbing mother—ricochet through stock situations that can be traced back to commedia dell'arte or to ancient Roman comedy. Virginia Higginbotham sees the play as a parody of the all-important concept of honor in Spanish Golden Age drama.[13] Lorca tied the play to Spanish tradition by subtitling it an "erotic alleluia": alleluias were cheap colored sheets published in the eighteenth century, telling little stories in sketches and doggerel. Eighteenth-century costume is specified in the play. Belisa's Mother, for example, wears a huge eighteenth-century wig decked out with birds, ribbons, and glass beads.

Lorca's brother Francisco García Lorca has further
noted that the four main characters "interweave their
voices in a kind of concerto grosso for four instruments.
Maybe none of Lorca's plays shows with more evidence
the musical influence in his theatre."[14]

Lorca's masterpiece of the folk-entertainment
genre is *The Shoemaker's Prodigious Wife*, a simple
farce in two acts that encompasses song, dance, slapstick violence, earthy humor, tender lyricism, and
philosophical intimations about the human need to balance reality with a dose of fantasy. Although a "chamber
version" of the play had been presented in 1930 by
Margarita Xirgu, Lorca said that the real premiere was
that of the expanded version of 1933, presented in Buenos Aires "with 18th- and 19th-century songs and
danced by the extraordinarily graceful Lola Membrives
and her company."[15] The published text of the play
contains two songs and a ballad which Lorca composed
almost as a parody of the ancient form while tying it
into the narrative thread of the plot.

"The language is of the people," Lorca wrote, "spoken in a Castilian accent, but with Andalusian vocabulary and syntax, allowing me at times—as when the
shoemakers's wife scolds—to employ a light Cervantes-
esque caricature."[16] Daniel Devoto notes that this play
contains the richest collection of folk locutions in contemporary Spanish literature; his article on "The Traditional Element in the Work of García Lorca" (*Filología*,
1950) lists over fifty examples.[17] Lorca said further:
"The concerned letters that I've received from my
friends in Paris who are involved in their beautiful and
bitter struggle with abstract art have impelled me to
write, in reaction, this tale which is almost vulgar in its
direct reality; I wanted an invisible thread of poetry to
flow through it and I wanted for the comic voice and
humor to stand out clearly and without false notes from
the beginning."[18]

The prologue to *The Shoemaker's Prodigious Wife*, spoken by the Author, emphasizes its popular sources: "Everywhere throbbing with vitality is the poetic being that the author has decked out with the air of a refrain or a simple little ballad as a shoemaker's wife."[19] The Author's polite speech is interrupted by the offstage shouts of the Shoemaker's Wife, impatient to make her entrance. Bidding the audience good night, the Author tips his hat, and a green light shines from inside it. As he reacts to that, water gushes from the hat and gets him wet. Embarrassed, he backs off stage, saying ironically "I beg your pardon." This sight gag operates on several levels. Robert Lima sees it as an homage to Buster Keaton, the Great Stone Face of silent film comedy.[20] In its apparent gratuitousness, it also serves as the kind of "circus trick" that periodically enlivened mystery plays to hold a popular audience's attention. On the other hand, it might be interpreted in relation to the final scene in *The Audience,* in which the Director (another incarnation of the Author) squares off with a Prestidigitator. The irony that the "bit" provokes in *The Shoemaker's Prodigious Wife* arises from the fact that the functions of the serious artist and the sleight-of-hand artist are both carried out by one character; it is as if Lorca were bemusedly acknowledging the writer's occasional need of cheap tricks in order to get his point across.

The action occurs in the house of the fifty-three-year-old Shoemaker and his eighteen-year-old Wife. There is a large window, to which the housebound little Wife is constantly drawn as she tries to feel a part of the colorful life of the street. The window also allows gossiping neighbors to eavesdrop on the marital discord in the house. Like Shakespeare's Kate in *The Taming of the Shrew,* the Wife probably became a hot-tempered scold largely in reaction to a deep psychological hurt. She is as quick to weep as she is to browbeat. Her tongue-lashings of her husband serve as a release for her pent-up vitality. She taunts her husband with glowing descriptions of the suitors she could have married. This is the aspect of her fantasy life to which Lorca referred in his 1933 comment on the play: "The Shoemaker's Wife struggles constantly with ideas and with actual objects, because she lives in her own little world where each idea and each object have a mysterious sense that she herself does not understand. She has never lived, nor has she ever had any suitors other than those on the opposite shore that she cannot and never will reach."[21]

The Wife intervenes to prevent the Shoemaker from being cheated in payment for his work; this embarrasses him and further antagonizes the customer, one of the gossiping neighbors. After the Wife storms out, the Shoemaker complains of his lot to the Mayor, who brags of the way he dealt with the four wives he has outlived: "The thing for women is to grab them tightly at the waist, give them a few swift kicks and orders shouted at the top of your voice, and if they still dare to crow at you, then the stick is the only answer."[22] The Shoemaker confides that he intends to run away, even though it means abandoning his home and business.

Don Mirlo (or Don Blackbird) comes to the window when the Wife is alone and tries to make an assignation with her, but she slaps him and sends him away. She is more receptive to the sweet talk of a Youth with a Sash, but when he goes too far she slams the window down. She wants only to talk to someone, but "in this town it's one extreme or the other: be a nun or a scrub."[23] She rushes offstage to check on the dinner she had threatened not to cook for the Shoemaker. Then he creeps out, dressed for traveling, carrying a bundle of clothes. Encountering two Pious Women at his doorway, he realizes that the news of his going will soon be all over town.

Only one person in the village seems to bring out the best in the Shoemaker's Wife, and that is the Little Boy. He has been sent by the neighbors to give the Wife the news about her husband's departure, but before he can tell her, he is distracted by a butterfly that enters through the window. He sings, as if to charm it, and then together the Boy and the Wife chase the butterfly about the room. Lorca's mature theatrical sensibilities are well displayed in this lyrical interlude, exactly the change of pace needed in the action at this point. The butterfly chase places the Wife on the same plane as the innocent child, establishing her basic innocence. The sequence underscores Lorca's theme of fantasy trapped by reality, for the butterfly is a fanciful image inside the house. As a symbol, the butterfly might represent the Wife in that it is brighter than its surroundings, or the Shoemaker in that it finally escapes through the door. The Boy follows the butterfly out, calling out his message as he goes. The Wife is stunned. Immediately, the house is overrun with neighbors who had been lurking outside. They swirl about "with the liveliness and rhythm of a dance," offering refreshments with mock sympathy. The Wife's loud sobs are heard above all the excitement as the act ends.

Act 2 occurs four months later. The Wife has opened a tavern in the house to support herself. Don Mirlo and the Youth with a Sash patronize her business, but the Wife is not interested in flirting with them; she declares her fidelity to her husband until death. The little Boy comes to visit. He got hurt when he defended the Wife's reputation against villagers who were singing an indecent song about her. It becomes clear that the neighbor women are jealous because so many men visit her tavern. The Mayor is her next visitor. He poses as her protector, but he too makes indecent propositions. She spurns him angrily, but the tension is broken by the sound of a puppet show's

arrival in the village. The Wife becomes childlike with
excitement when the traveling entertainer comes into her tavern.

The villagers crowd in to hear him recite a ballad.
The narrative so closely resembles the Wife's own story
that she bursts into tears and hiccups. Just as he
reaches the climax of his tale, shouts are heard offstage.
A neighbor reports that several young men are fighting
with knives over the Wife.

Everyone rushes off, leaving the Wife alone with
the minstrel, whom she does not recognize as the Shoemaker. She breaks down in sobs and tells him how hard
it is to live alone, constantly having to defend herself
from unwanted suitors and vicious gossips. When he
suggests that her husband was irresponsible in abandoning her, she defends the Shoemaker and even
builds him up to fantastical proportions. The minstrel
then confesses that he left his wife and now regrets it.
When he tries to proposition her, she puts him in his
place. Meanwhile, excitement is mounting in the
street, for blood has been drawn and the whole town
blames it on the Wife. She valiantly prepares to defend
herself. The Shoemaker, about to depart, asks what he
should say if by chance he should meet her husband in
his travels. She says to tell him that she loves him and
thinks him more attractive than any younger man and
would treat him like a king if only he would return. The
Shoemaker removes his disguise. They embrace deliri-
ously. Just then voices from the street begin singing the
indecent song about the Wife. She reacts by blaming it
all on her husband. As she begins shrewishly calling
him names, he goes happily to his cobbler's bench. The
play ends as she yells through the window to her neighbors: "Come on, come ahead now if you like. Now
there are two of us to defend the house, two! two! me
and my husband. That rascal, that scoundrel!"[24]

In a 1933 interview about the formation of theatre

clubs to bring art within the reach of everyone, Lorca described *The Shoemaker's Prodigious Wife* as "a farce that is also a poetic example of the human soul." He said, too, that "the shoemaker's wife is not a particular woman, but all women. All audience members carry a shoemaker's wife caged in their breasts."[25] The play is, as Lorca intended, Andalusian in rhythm and color, but universal in substance.

Lorca's most intensive and rewarding contact with Spanish folk life came about through his work with *La Barraca*, the itinerant theatre group he founded in 1932 to take theatre to rural areas of Spain. The idea came to Lorca on November 1, 1931, after he had attended a Madrid performance of José Zorrilla's *Don Juan Tenorio*, which is traditionally presented throughout Spain every year on All Soul's Day. Lorca was angered by the unimaginative staging and uninspired acting of that masterpiece of Spanish Romanticism, which is set in Spain's seventeenth-century Golden Age. This incited him to conceive with missionarylike zeal a project that would revitalize the Spanish theatre, and he hurried to the Morla Lynch home to talk about it. Carlos Morla Lynch recalled that occasion:

In the middle of the night, Federico bursts into the social gathering with the impetuosities of a whirlwind. He comes in extremely vibrant, exalted, caught up in a euphoria that his unbridled outpouring spreads to us by contagion. . . . It has to do with a new idea that has spurted forth with the violence of an eruption in his constantly effervescent spirit. A seductive vision of vast proportions: to construct a *barraca* (hut) with the capacity for 400 people, for the purpose of "saving the Spanish theatre" and putting it within reach of the people. In this shed will be presented works of Calderón de la Barca, Lope de Vega, plays of Cervantes, etc. . . . "La Barraca" will be portable. A theatre that is itinerant and free, that will travel the parched highways of Castile, the dusty roads of Andalusia, all the routes that cross the Spanish countryside. To make its way into the small settlements, villages, and ham-

lets, and it will set up its stage and miniature properties in
the small plazas. A resurrection of the itinerant *farándula*
(strolling players) of olden times. Cooperation of Manuel
Ugarte, a great friend of Federico, like him, full of altruistic
projects, an impulsive organizer of cultural crusades trans-
versing small towns and settlements.[26]

When Morla Lynch asked where the funds for this mag-
nificent project would come from, Lorca replied: "That
will be taken care of later. Those are mere details."

Luckily, the time was favorable for such a plan. After a series of popular elections in April 1931, Spain's
Second Republic was established. The Bourbon monarchy, which until 1930 had harbored the dictatorship of
Primo de Rivera, had come to an end with the exile of
King Alfonso XIII. The new Republican government
created a Ministry of Culture and Information to combat the illiteracy that existed in perhaps as much as 50
percent of the Spanish population, and to promote
a sense of national unity among the various regions
of Spain.[27] Lorca's proposal was strongly supported
by Fernando de los Ríos, who became minister of
public instruction in March 1932. That same month,
*La Barraca* was awarded a government subsidy of
100,000 pesetas.

Lorca chose the name *La Barraca,* because he envisioned a "little hut" on wheels. The company's em-
blem was a wheel with a mask at the center. This was
worn as a badge on the blue coveralls that Lorca chose
as a uniform to project a worker's image for the wearers
and establish a bond with *La Barraca's* audience of la-
borers. Lorca liked to wear the uniform when he gave
public lectures, and he occasionally even slept in it.[28]

The major initial expenses were the purchase of a
truck and the construction of a portable stage eight meters wide by six meters deep, and one meter in height.
The stage was curtained at the back and sides. Since
the stage was usually set up for open-air performance in

the town square, the troupe transported its own electrical lighting equipment. (Villagers were asked to bring their own chairs.) Sets and costumes were designed by various artists for each of the thirteen plays that were presented between July 1932 and April 1936 in seventy-four different towns and villages in Spain.[29] Because *La Barraca* was a government-subsidized, nonprofit venture, admission to performances was always free.

Lorca, his co-director Eduardo Ugarte, and the students who toured with *La Barraca* received no remuneration for their efforts; they were motivated at first by their idealism and later by the gratifying response of their audiences. In 1934, Lorca described the response he had witnessed repeatedly:

It is astonishing to see the thrill of pleasure, the close attention elicited from the villagers, who would strike anyone who made noise and caused them to miss a word. In what are apparently the most backward villages in Spain, they listen to our presentations, which are the most faithfully reconstructed versions of our classical theatre. . . . Our audiences, the true captives of theatrical art, are of two extremes: the cultivated classes, either university-educated or from other intellectual or spontaneously artistic backgrounds, and the common people, the poorest, least refined people, uncorrupted, naive, fertile ground for every shudder of sorrow and every sparkle of wit.[30]

Often, audience members responded to the performances with shouts of "Viva España!"[31]

Actors and stagehands were recruited from among university students in Madrid. After an interview with Lorca and Ugarte and perhaps one or two other organizers of the undertaking, students went through a four-step audition process, presenting selections in both prose and poetry. Rehearsals were held at the *Residencia de Estudiantes*, and the productions toured during summer vacations. Although their personalities were as

different as could be from one another, Lorca and
Ugarte worked well together. Lorca was the ubiquitous
stage director; he adapted the Golden Age texts, conceived the production styles, arranged the incidental
music, oversaw the design elements, and worked
closely with the actors. The owlish Ugarte functioned as
a critical observer and a check on Lorca's extravagant
impulses; Lorca said of him: "He is always right."

Directing stage productions was invaluable experience for Lorca as a playwright. His success as a director
might be measured by the positive recollections of
those who worked with him as well as by audience response. He seemed to have a sixth sense for casting the
right actor in each role. According to Luís Sáenz de la
Calzada, he directed individual actors in different ways,
in response to the needs of each "not intuitively, but
with great certainty." He also required that his actors
learn not only their own roles, but the entire work, because he felt that "the melody could be established only
when all the notes were on the musical staff."[32] He was
meticulous about timing: a second's delay in making an
entrance could throw off the rhythm of a stage performance as disastrously as an instrument coming in at the
wrong time in a symphony.[33] Lorca's artistic intransi-
gence did not, however, turn his actors into "supermar-
ionettes." Mechanical responses and affectation were
not tolerated; Lorca insisted upon honesty of characterization as the basis for exaggerated forms like farce.

Vocal quality and diction were of primary importance to Lorca, but he also paid close attention to gesture. In the four *entremeses* by Cervantes that he
staged, Lorca called for a stylized exaggeration of gesture. He incorporated pantomime into Calderón de la
Barca's *Life is a Dream* (*La Vida es sueño*). C. Rivas
Cherif says that Lorca's artistic intention was to bring
out the poetic values of that work through a "very fluid
scenic interpretation, closer to the pure evocative plas-

ticity of ballet than to direct dramatic emotion in which
spontaneity is feigned." One of Lorca's actresses recalled that all of his stage blocking approached choreog-
raphy.[34] According to Lorca's sister Isabel García
Lorca, who toured with *La Barraca,* "the really modern
aspect of Lorca's theatrical technique lay in his power
to impart a true spirit of life and motion to the stage.
This renovative influence was apparent in the sets, the
costumes, the lighting, and especially in the players'
mannerisms and gestures on stage."[35]

On July 10, 1932, *La Barraca* departed from Madrid on the first of its twenty-two excursions over the
next four years. The first performance took place that
evening in the medieval town of Burgo de Osma. On
the portable stage set up in the medieval town's main
square, three *entremeses* by Miguel de Cervantes were
presented to an enthusiastic audience. The same program was offered on the four successive evenings in
four other towns. Then Lorca's adaptation of Calderón
de la Barca's *Life is a Dream* with musical accompaniment was put into the repertoire. Lorca played the Shadow in that allegorical work; it was the only role he
ever performed with *La Barraca,* although he often accompanied the tours. His more usual function was to
improvise a prologue before the performance, establishing a rapport between performers and audiences, explaining what they were about to see and how it related
to their own rich cultural heritage. He would sit unob-
trusively in the audience during performances, watch-
ing reactions that would guide him in choosing and
adapting other works for the repertoire.

Lorca never exploited *La Barraca* to enhance his
own reputation. When he addressed audiences directly,
he remained anonymous. None of his own plays was
ever presented by *La Barraca.* The repertoire was
mostly Golden Age drama, including Lope de Vega's
*Sheep's Well (Fuenteovejuna)* and *The Knight from*

Olmedo (*El Caballero de Olmedo*). The only modern
work ever presented was a stage adaptation of a traditionally inspired narrative ballad by Antonio Machado.

Lorca's own reward for the venture, apart from altruistic gratifications, was experience itself: close observation of how a play works in performance and of what
makes an audience respond with laughter or tears or
fear or exultation. His ability to adapt Golden Age
drama for modern audiences was put to use again later
when he adapted Lope de Vega's *The Silly Lady* (*La
Dama boba*) for presentation by Lola Membrives's company in Buenos Aires in 1933. It should be noted that
Lorca insisted that he had not really adapted, but only
abridged Lope de Vega's work, for "masterpieces cannot be revised. That is a sin I would never dare to com-
mit."[36] These experiences reinforced Lorca's instinct
for simplified texts with strong lyrical elements, and
prepared him in the surest possible way to write his
dramatic masterpieces.

In 1934 *La Barraca*'s subsidy was cut in half, but it
continued to tour and to add new productions to the
repertoire, including Tirso de Molina's *The Trickster of
Seville* (*El Burlador de Sevilla*), the original seventeenth-century Don Juan play. By 1935 *La Barraca* was
beginning to be hampered by financial difficulties and
political tensions.[37] Its last performances were given as
part of a theatre festival in Barcelona in April 1936. In
its four-year existence, *La Barraca* made a lasting impression on twentieth-century Spanish culture. "Truly,"
writes Suzanne Byrd in her book on the subject, "La
Barraca was the embryo of Spain's now flourishing national theatre."[38] It was not only a source of entertainment for rural populations that had never before seen
live theatre, but it also aroused their intellectual,
moral, and patriotic sensibilities. Finally, it reestab-
lished the dramatic viability of Spanish Golden Age
drama.

# 6

~~~~~~~~~~~~~~~~~~~~~~~~~~~~~~~~~~~~~~~~~~~~~~~~

# New Directions in Poetry

Lorca's mature poems are collected under four titles: *Poet in New York* (*Poeta en Nueva York*, written 1929–1930, published 1940), *Lament for Ignacio Sánchez Mejías* (*Llanto por Ignacio Sánchez Mejías*, 1935), *Six Galician Poems* (*Seis poemas galegos*, 1935), and *Divan of the Tamarit* (*Diván del Tamarit*, written 1936, published 1941); in addition, some of Lorca's uncollected poems (*poemas sueltos*) are from his mature period. If Lorca's artistic development is seen as a progression toward synthesis of all the arts, this mature poetry might at first glance appear to deviate from that convergence of music, visual art, and poetic expression that gave rise to his full-blown theatrical artistry. However, it is important to recall that the period of this poetry is also that which produced his most experimental work for the theatre: *The Audience* (1930), *When Five Years Pass* (1931), and *Play without a Title* (1935). Juxtaposition of these plays with *Poet in New York*, Lorca's most hermetic group of poems, suggests that Lorca was either intentionally or subconsciously obscuring his newly unfettered subjectivity of content by the unconventionality of the forms in which he couched his preoccupations. After thus testing the limits of subjective content and experimental form, he could pull back from those extremes and write with the confident grace of one who has truly mastered his art: the return to lyri-

cism of *Divan of the Tamarit* is effected with unprecedented sophistication of poetic vision, just as the return
to conventional plotting and characterization in his last
plays, *Doña Rosita the Spinster* and *The House of Bernarda Alba,* is accomplished without sacrifice of heightened theatricality in the use of scenic metaphor.

*Poet in New York* may be tied in several ways to
Lorca's development as a dramatist. José Ortega suggests that these poems represent a preliminary phase in
Lorca's desire to achieve the artistic transformation of a
chaotic, brutal, materialistic society, and that this concern necessitated "the multivalent perspective and
broader communicative system" of the theatre.[1] Derek
Harris writes of the conflict of values that is central to
this book[2] and of the dominance of malignant forces:
"The conflict makes him a dramatic poet, and the une-
qual stature of the combatants makes him a tragic
poet."[3] Betty Jean Craige sees these poems as emblematic of a "fall into consciousness" through separation
from nature; they document a poet's journey from
alienation to regained harmony with the universe, exemplified by the musicality of the final two poems after
the disjointed rhythms of most of the work.[4] Since
drama is the most objective of literary genres, the consciousness with which *Poet in New York* was composed
serves, along with the movement and dramatic reversal
contained in the work as a whole, as evidence of Lorca's
increasing tendency to write in a dramatic mode.

*Poet in New York* is, as Richard Predmore points
out, not as much about New York as it is about the
poet's own psychological state while he was in New
York and elsewhere in America.[5] Lorca had come to
New York hoping that the journey would distract him
from a severe emotional crisis. During his Atlantic
crossing he wrote to Carlos Morla Lynch: "I don't know
why I left; I ask myself a hundred times a day. I look at
myself in the mirror of the close little cabin and don't

recognize myself. I seem to be another Federico."[6] (The first poem in the collection refers to "coming upon my face that's different every day.") New York immersed Lorca in a culture that was as different from Andalusia as could possibly be. Lorca's acclimatization was impeded by his inability to speak or understand English. According to Angel del Río, who befriended Lorca at that time, "whatever significance *Poet in New York* may have does not spring from any genuine contact with actual American life, which the poet saw only from the outside."[7]

The first of the ten sections of *Poet in New York* is entitled "Poems of Solitude at Columbia University," and it comprises four poems about the poet's present disorientation and about his nostalgia for the past and for childhood innocence. The first poem, "Return from a Walk" (*Vuelta de paseo*), contains in its twelve lines some of the most striking images in the book: "assassinated by the sky," "the child with the white face of an egg," "the stump-limbed tree that doesn't sing," "tiny animals with broken heads," "tattered water of dry feet," "butterfly drowned in the inkwell," and "my face that's different every day." The second poem is entitled "1910," the year when Lorca was twelve; it recalls what kinds of things his eyes did and did not see at that time, and ends with the observation that his vision has lost its innocent literalness: "I have seen that things seeking their course find their own vacancy." (*He visto que las cosas / cuando buscan su curso encuentran su vacío.*)

"Fable and Round of the Three Friends" (*Fabula y rueda de los tres amigos*) uses the structure and repetitions of a children's circle game. The three friends may be three different aspects of the poet's persona: the sensualist "frozen . . . in the world of beds," the working artist "in the world of eyes and wounded hands," and the dreamer "in the world of universities without roofs." The sufferings of the three friends, who are "burnèd," "buried," "grasped in my hands," and "mummified," might allude to the psychological anguish of the published poet, who won applause after he "killed the fifth moon" (published his fifth book of poetry, *Gypsy Ballad,* the success of which was a factor in Lorca's depressed mood in 1928–1929). Derek Harris goes on to suggest that the "sixth moon" mentioned at the end of the poem might refer to the eventual publication of *Poet in New York*.[8] The poet understood that he "had been murdered" when "pure forms were overwhelmed by the *cri cri* of daisies." By "pure forms" Lorca probably meant poetry as he performed it for live audiences, while the flowery tributes that followed publication of a poem represent a kind of death. The poem continues: "They destroyed three skeletons to extract their gold teeth. / Still they didn't find me." (*Destrozaron tres esqueletos para arrancar sus dientes de oro./ Ya no me encontraron*.) Those who make a cult of the poet's art may tear apart—or analyze—the very bones of his various personae, but they will never fully understand his creative spirit.

The second section of *Poet in New York,* entitled "The Blacks," comprises three poems, the first two of which reflect Harlem's fascination for Lorca. He described it in his "Lecture on New York" as "the most important black city in the world, where lewdness has a touch of innocence that makes it unsettling and religious."[9] In the long poem "The King of Harlem" (*El Rey de Harlem*), African animals and other tropical or primitive images are set in opposition to the hard metallic objects of white civilization. For example, the opening stanza is:

> With a spoon
> he dug out the eyes of crocodiles
> and spanked the monkeys' rumps.
> With a spoon.

> *Con una cuchara*
> *arrancaba los ojos a los cocodrilos*
> *y golpeaba el trasero de los monos.*
> *Con una cuchara.*[10]

The spoon might be equated with Lorca's reference to the fork in his lecture on these poems: "I wanted to write the poem of the black race in North America and to put emphasis on the pain that the blacks experience for being black in a contrary world; slaves of all of the white man's inventions and machines, with the perpetual fear that one day they may forget how to light the gas stove or steer the car or fasten the starched collar, or that they may stick the fork in an eye."[11] Thus, the opening stanza of "The King of Harlem" shows the black king using the white man's implement to overcome his African heritage. In the course of the poem, however, the primitive vitality of the blacks—symbolized by gushing, pervasive blood imagery—overwhelms and encompasses the detritus of the sterile city. The irregular rhythms are punctuated by several lines of incantatory value like "¡Ay, Harlem! ¡Ay, Harlem! ¡Ay, Harlem!" and "Negros, Negros, Negros, Negros."

African animal imagery abounds also in "Dance of Death" (*Danza de la muerte*), in which an African mask comes to New York, and a jungle smothers Wall Street. That poem opens the section entitled "Streets and Dreams," which includes several grim, subjective visions of the hostile city. "Landscape of the Vomiting Multitude" (*Paisaje de la multitud que vomita*) is subtitled "Coney Island Twilight"; its stress on seemingly unrelated objects and its crowd, represented by an implacably advancing fat woman, evoke the loneliness described in Lorca's lecture: "You cannot imagine the loneliness that a Spaniard feels there, especially one from the south. Because if you fall you will be trampled, and if you slip and fall in the water, they will toss

papers from their lunches onto you."[12] Metaphors of
dehumanization occur also in "Landscape of the Urinating Multitudes" (*Paisaje de la multitud que orina*), subtitled "Battery Place Nocturne," and in "Christmas on
the Hudson" (*Navidad en el Hudson*). Many images are
similar to those in Lorca's drawings; in "Sleepless City;
Brooklyn Bridge Nocturne" (*Ciudad sin sueño*), for example, he says: "Kisses bind mouths together in a tan-
gle of newborn veins." (*Los besos atan las bocas / en
una maraña de venas recientes*.)

The fourth through sixth sections of *Poet in New
York*, "Poems from Lake Eden Mills," "In the Farmer's
Cabin," and "Introduction to Death; Poems of Solitude
in Vermont," were inspired by the pastoral setting and
rural folk that Lorca encountered during his stay with
Phillip Cummings at Lake Eden in Vermont. Although
in these sections the poet's anguish seems less acute
and the word "empty," or "emptiness," no longer crops
up in every poem, one is nonetheless aware of the presence of death in the poet's consciousness. In "Double
Poem of Lake Eden" (*Poema doble del Lago Eden*), he
weeps "because I am not a man, nor a poet, nor a leaf, /
but a wounded pulse that probes what is on the other
side." (*porque yo no soy un hombre, ni un poeta, ni
una hoja, / pero sí un pulso herido que sonda las cosas
del otro lado*.)[13] Even a ten-year-old boy, in "Little
Boy Stanton" (*El Niño Stanton*), reminded Lorca that
death comes to all living things: "Your ten years will be
the leaves / that flutter on the clothing of the dead." (*Tu
diez años serán las hojas / que vuelan en los trajes de
los muertos*."[14] Stanton's little sister Mary fell into a
well and was drowned during Lorca's stay there, and he
was reminded of a similar drowning in Granada many
years earlier. In his imagination the two little girls became one, crying as she fell, striking her head against
the inner walls of the well. Lorca expressed his deep
sorrow in the poem "Little Girl Drowned in the Well;

Granada and Newburg," whose haunting refrain—
"water that never flows free" (*agua que no desemboca*)—echoes through each stanza like a voice echoing in a well.

Among the numerous shared motifs of *Poet in New York* and Lorca's 1930 play *The Audience* are the Mask (in "Dance of Death"), an octopus turned inside out (in "Landscape of the Vomiting Multitude), a dead fish (in "Abandoned Church"), a white horse with a mane of ashes (in "Nocturne of the Void"), arches, stairways, apples, worms, veins, cancer, ink, ants, and sand. As it recurs in various poems, the image of sand seems to connote a permeable layering of levels of consciousness; this would accord with the metaphor of the wall of sand that separates "true theatre" from commercial theatre in *The Audience*. Like *The Audience*, *Poet in New York* contains a transformation sequence; in "Death" (*Muerte*), animals and objects strain to become something else until finally the poet, too, undergoes a metamorphosis, becoming a "seraph of flames."

Section 7 of *Poet in New York*, "Return to the City," contains the poet's direct denunciation of New York in a poem entitled "New York: Office and Denunciation" (*New York: Oficina y Denuncia*). Lorca knew what frenetic and mechanical rhythms to expect of the city on his return there. His matter-of-fact repetitions of sounds, phrases, and rhythms give an incantatory quality to his litany of accusations: the millions of animals butchered each day, the Hudson drunk on oil, half the population cemented over by the other half.

The first of the "Two Odes" in Section 8 is "Cry unto Rome" (*Grito hacía Roma*), which was apparently provoked by the signing of the Papal Concordat with Mussolini in February 1929.[15] Religious symbols are juxtaposed with images of violence and corrupt materialism. A close analysis of the poem by Derek Harris demonstrates that it is a curse on the Church of Rome for its apparent indifference to human suffering, and it culminates in an inversion of the sense of the Lord's Prayer.[16] The second poem in this section is the relatively long "Ode to Walt Whitman." Angel del Río has written of the possible influence of Whitman's poetry on Lorca and of Lorca's friendship in New York with León Felipe, the translator of Whitman's poems into Spanish.[17] The ode begins by referring to various groups of young men in the city, whose lives are devoid of romantic vision. Then Lorca describes their opposite:

> Not for a moment, beautiful old Walt Whitman,
> have I stopped seeing your beard full of butterflies.

> *Ni un solo momento, viejo hermoso Walt Whitman,*
> *he dejado de ver tu barba llena de mariposas.*[18]

Whitman is eulogized for the virility and dignity behind his pure sensory appreciation of beauty, while Whitman's homosexuality attains a kind of nobility by contrast to that of the male sissies who inhabit every large city.

On leaving New York, Lorca abandoned the jarring rhythms and harsh images of his city poems. Although the three poems of the book's last two sections mark a return to musicality, they are still closer in spirit to the rest of *Poet in New York* than to Lorca's earlier poetry. "Flight from New York; Two Waltzes toward Civilization" is composed of two poems whose impulse toward innocence and nostalgia is checked by little reminders of death imbedded in the seductive sound and rhythmic patterns. The love that is evoked in "Little Viennese Waltz" (*Pequeño vals vienés*) is fixed in the past like a snapshot, but remembered through a nostalgic haze like a dream of old Vienna or Hungary: "Take this waltz that dies away in my arms." (*Toma este vals que se muere en mis brazos.*) The poem ends:

> and in the dark waves of your going
> I want to leave, my love, my love,
> violin and sepulchre, the measure of the waltz.

> *y en las ondas oscuras de tu andar*
> *quiero, amor mío, amor mío, dejar*
> *violín y sepulcro, las cintas del vals.*[19]

"Waltz in the Branches" (*Vals en las ramas*), the penultimate poem in the book, recalls "Fable and Round of the Three Friends" of the opening section, in that both are written in the form of children's singing games. This "Waltz" also refers to "three," but the three are no longer corporeal beings. They fall as leaves from a tree, like flesh from a skeleton, leaving "hard ivory" (the moon) caught in the branches. A second reference to ivory, now used in the plural, occurs in the last line of the poem and brings in an overlapping image of piano keys:

| | |
|---|---|
| One by one | *Una a una* |
| around the moon | *alrededor de la luna,* |
| two by two | *dos a dos* |
| around the sun, | *alrededor del sol,* |
| and three by three | *y tres a tres* |
| so that the ivories fall | *para que los marfiles* |
| sound asleep. | *se duerman bien.*[20] |

A single poem falls under the heading "The Poet Arrives in Havana." The irresistible spell cast by black and Latin cultures in Cuba is evoked in "Sound of the Blacks in Cuba" (*Son de negros en Cuba*), with its mesmerizing refrain of every other line: "I'll go to Santiago" (*Iré a Santiago*). Still, the mood is not entirely upbeat. The poet had been too profoundly marked by his New York experience:

| | |
|---|---|
| The sea drowned in sand, | *El mar ahogado en la arena,* |
| I'll go to Santiago, | *iré a Santiago,* |
| white heat, decayed fruit, | *calor blanco, fruta muerta,* |
| I'll go to Santiago. | *iré a Santiago.*[21] |

Lorca's most sustained meditation on death is his *Lament for Ignacio Sánchez Mejías,* which most critics consider his greatest achievement as a lyric poet. This deeply felt tribute to his friend, who died after the fourth *corrida* of his return to the bullring following a seven-year retirement, combines traditional features of elegiac form with a modern sensibility in the choice of images. It exemplifies Lorca's continuing progression toward a synthesis of the arts by its four-movement musical structure, by the pictorial clarity with which the toreador, the bull, and the blood on the sand are sketched, and by the dramatic tension sustained between the color and violence of the action in the bullring and the stark, silent emptiness of the *corrida*'s aftermath. Edwin Honig declares that *"Llanto por Ignacio Sánchez Mejías* is the work of a poet in whose consciousness dramatic and poetic forms have interpenetrated."[22]

Marcelle Auclair, who was a friend of both Lorca and Sánchez Mejías, states that the *Lament* is entirely factual in its narrative content: Lorca's inventiveness lay in the poetic means by which he heightened the descriptive content.[23] She recalls a day in the spring of 1934 when Lorca's friends were gathered to celebrate his return from South America; he arrived, distraught, and said: "Ignacio has just announced his own death to me: he's going back to the bullring."[24] The entire poem is permeated with that sense of fatality by which, according to Edward F. Stanton, "the destinies of the bull and the matador are bound together."[25] Auclair and numerous friends of Sánchez Mejías were present at the forty-three-year-old matador's first return performance on August 5, 1934, at Santander, where Lorca's touring theatre, *La Barraca,* was scheduled to perform a few days later. Sánchez Mejías's work with the two bulls he killed that day was brilliant and heart-stopping in its audacity and beauty. He mentioned afterward that he had three contracts to fill—on August 6, 10, and 12—after which he would retire definitively.[26]

Shortly after his August 10 engagement, Sánchez

Mejías received a message asking him to serve as a last-minute replacement on the program at Manzanares on August 11. Although he would have preferred to refuse, his pride forced him to accept the invitation whose subtext was a taunting challenge. At Manzanares, the accommodations provided him were so poor that he almost left, but was deterred by his assistant's remark that the bulls were enormous and high-horned: it might be said that Sánchez Mejías was afraid. For the first time in his bullfighting career, Sánchez Mejías participated directly in the drawing for the assignment of the bulls; with his own hand he drew the paper on which the bull's name, Granadino, was written. He noted that the local infirmary appeared substandard and ordered that if anything should happen to him he was to be taken to Madrid by ambulance. Sánchez Mejías had asked to be first on the program so that he could leave as soon as possible for his engagement at Pontevedra the next day. He entered the ring at five o'clock.[27] While executing a daring pass of the *muleta* with his back against the inside of the ring where there is no margin for error, Sánchez Mejías was gored in the left thigh and groin; the horn penetrated his abdomen, and his blood spattered nearby spectators. A superficial disinfectant was applied on the spot, the smell of which Lorca evokes in the first movement of his *Lament*, entitled "The Fatal Wound and Death."[28]

The ambulance broke down en route to Madrid and did not arrive until the morning of August 12.[29] There, Lorca kept close contact with the doctors who tried vainly for a full day to save Sánchez Mejías. Lorca telephoned hourly reports to his friends in Santander and finally, grief-striken, reported that Sánchez Mejías had died at 9:45 A.M. on August 13.[30] In the second movement of the *Lament*, "The Spilled Blood," Lorca repeats six times, plus several times with variations, the line "I don't want to see it!" (¡*Que no quiero verla!*), referring to the bullfighter's blood. Marcelle Auclair affirms that he never went into the room where his friend lay dying, nor did he visit the candlelit chapel where the body lay in state.[31] Lorca could envision those things clearly enough to write the third movement entitled "The Display of the Body." The Spanish title of that movement, *"Cuerpo presente"* (literally, "the present body"), which is the term used for a laid-out body in a chapel, sets up a contrast with the title of the fourth movement, "Absent Soul." Lorca began writing his *Lament for Ignacio Sánchez Mejías* in September and read it publicly for the first time on March 12, 1935, at the Teatro Español in Madrid on the occasion of the one-hundredth performance of *Yerma*.

Undoubtedly, the most familiar line in the *Lament* is the insistently reiterated "At five o'clock in the afternoon" (*A los cinco de la tarde*), comprising every other line of the first movement. The very monotony reinforces the poem's aura of fatality. A recording of the poem by Germaine Montero (Vanguard VRS 9055) spellbindingly conveys all the helplessness and anguish expressed by the obsessive repetition of that simple line. William Carlos Williams says that "the stress on the first syllable of the 'CINco' is the pure sound of a barbaric music, the heartbeat of a man's song, *A las CINco de la tarde*."[32] The effect of the entire movement is to expand time, as Lorca did in the first act of his play *When Five Years Pass*. The sounds, smells, and impressions made on the crowd of spectators as well as those flashing through the mind of the bullfighter at five o'clock in the afternoon are dissected, broken down into their separate components. Two lines will exemplify that juxtaposition of objective and subjective impressions: "The wind carried off bits of cotton" (*El viento se llevó los algodónes*) and "The bull was bellowing now through his forehead" (*El toro ya mugía por su frente*).

The second movement is the action sequence. Despite the poet's refusal to see the blood, he compulsively recreates those terrible moments: "His eyes did not close / when he saw the horns close by." (*No se cerraron sus ojos / cuando vió los cuernos cerca*.) This section also evokes the bullfighter's courage, skill, physical attractiveness, and warmth of personality. He entered the ring confidently "shouldering all of his death" (*con toda su muerte a cuestas*). Then his blood flows

> like a long, dark, sad tongue
> to form a puddle of agony
> beside the Guadalquivir of the stars.
> Oh, white wall of Spain!
> Oh, black bull of sorrow!
> Oh, hard blood of Ignacio!
> Oh, nightingale of his veins!
> No.
> I don't want to see it!

> *como una larga, oscura, triste lengua,*
> *para formar un charco de agonía*
> *junto al Guadalquivir de las estrellas.*
> *¡Oh blanco muro de España!*
> *¡Oh negro toro de pena!*
> *¡Oh sangre dura de Ignacio!*
> *¡Oh ruiseñor de sus venas!*
> *No.*
> *¡Que no quiero verla!*[23]

The rhythm slows in the third movement. The stillness surrounding "The Display of the Body" is reinforced by several references to "stone," which Lorca may have evoked for its permanence, but also because —according to Marcelle Auclair—Lorca was thinking of the stone slabs that served as operating tables in old arenas and as tables for cadavers in morgues. He was fascinated by the mystery of death:

> I want them to show me the way out
> for this captain tied down by death.

*Yo quiero que me enseñan dónde está la salida*
*para este capitán atado por la muerte.*[34]

The last movement seems to be distanced in time, place, and sentiment from all that is described earlier in the poem. Four four-line stanzas enumerate various animate and inanimate objects that do not know Sánchez Mejías "because you are dead for always" (*porque te has muerto para siempre*). Then a five-line stanza sets him in contrast to "all the dead of the Earth" in that the poet sings of his "appetite for death and the taste of its mouth" (*tu apetencia de muerte y el gusto de su boca*); it is hinted that the poet's song confers immortality.

The last two lines of the *Lament* are:

I sing of his elegance with groaning words,
and remember a sad breeze through olive trees.

*Yo canto su elegancia con palabras que gimen*
*y recuerdo una brisa triste por los olivos.*[35]

Marcelle Auclair reveals the little-known meaning of those lines: she and Lorca consoled each other by remembering good times they had spent with Sánchez Mejías. Once, in the early hours of the morning, after a night of dancing in cabarets, in a pensive mood Sánchez Mejías had spoken to them of his childhood: "At sixteen, without my father's knowledge, I went so far as to wave a red cape in front of some poor little cows on a ranch where I had made friends. I was proud of my passes, only sorry not to have an audience. And then when a hint of breeze stirred the olive trees, I raised my hand and acknowledged the applause."[36]

Death is the unifying theme of Lorca's *Six Galician Poems* (*Seis poemas galegos*), written in 1932 and published in 1935. Little critical commentary has been published on them, since they are written in the Galician language. A melancholy tone is established in the first poem "Madrigal to the City of Santiago" (*Madrigal a cibdá de Santiago*), with its references to nocturnal rain, silver grasses, moon, and sea. "Ballad of Our Lady of the Boat" (*Romaxe de nosa Señora da barca*) evokes the presence of death in the thronging crowds of a holy-day procession. According to Miguel García Posada, "Song of the Shop Boy" (*Cantiga do neno da tenda*) is about a young Galician exiled in Buenos Aires, who finally commits suicide in the Río de Plata; similarly, a drowned youth is the subject of "Nocturne of the Dead Youth" (*Noiturnio do adoescente morto*).[37] Grasses, wind, and sea are again associated with death in "Lulla-bye for the Dead Rosalia de Castro" (*Canzon de cuna pra Rosalia Castro, morta*). The lively couplets of "Dance of the Moon in Santiago" (*Danza da lúa en Santiago*) describe the moon, its "spent body" "dancing in the Courtyard of the Dead."[38]

Although death is a continuing preoccupation in *Divan of the Tamarit*, the elegance and grace with which it is treated in these poems suggest that the poet has achieved some philosophical distance on the subject of his deepest fear. The erotic passion that surfaces in certain of the poems is similarly muted—or transmuted into an aesthetically ordered memory of passion. The tone may be compared to that of Lorca's penultimate play, *Doña Rosita the Spinster*, with its mellow blend of nostalgia, sense of loss, and acceptance. After ventur-ing into uncharted territory with *Poet in New York* and *The Audience*, Lorca found that, figuratively, he could go home again to the lush, enclosed garden of Granada, where *Doña Rosita* is set and where the imprint of Ara-bic culture was a pervasive poetic influence.

The words *diván* and *Tamarit* both have several meanings. In the most likely sense, a *diván* is a collec-tion of poems (as in Goethe's *East-West Divan*), and *Tamarit* is the Arabic name for a garden property near Granada owned by relatives of Lorca. Edwin Honig ex-plains that "the Tamarit was the chief administrative of-fice of Arabic power in Spain during the period of Moorish domination. The *Diván* was the Arabic name for the assembly of governors who came periodically to hold council with the Tamarit. *Diván* also has another meaning: 'reunion.' And it is probably in this sense that Lorca intended it. By celebrating the spirit of all southern Spain, he sought to come to a 'reunion' with his past."[39] Miguel García Posada adds that Tamarit seems also to have been the name of a Nazarene poet.[40] Lorca designated the twenty-one poems in the collection as either *gacelas* or *casidas*, but did not adhere strictly to their Arabic forms.

The first poem, "Gacela of Unforeseen Love" (*Gacela del amor imprevisto*), entwines such already familiar objects as the moon, horses, jasmine, night, and a branch; and it ends:

> the blood of your veins in my mouth,
> your mouth now without light for my death.

> *la sangre de tus venas en mi boca,*
> *tu boca ya sin luz para mi muerte.*[41]

Although this vocabulary and the thematic focus on love and death can be traced back to Lorca's earliest work, there is here a post–New York sophistication in the use of metaphor:

> Between plaster and jasmines, your glance
> was a pale branch of seeds.

> *Entre yeso y jazmines, tu mirada*
> *era un pálido ramo de simientes.*[42]

The sensual connotations of "night" and "darkness" now seem to outweigh the hostile attributes that were more characteristic of Lorca's earlier poetry. Now comparatively at ease with his homosexuality, Lorca was also more willing to accept the transitory nature of existence: "four nights," "your always elusive body," "my death." This seems apparent also in the second of the four stanzas of "Gacela of the Flight" (*Gacela de la huida*):

There is not a night when, on giving a kiss,
one doesn't sense the smile of faceless people,
nor is there anyone who, on touching an infant,
forgets the unmoving skulls of horses.

*No hay noche que, al dar un beso,*
*no siento la sonrisa de las gentes sin rostro,*
*ni hay nadie que, al tocar un recién nacido,*
*olvide las inmóviles calaveras de caballos.*[43]

If the characteristic movement of the poems in *Divan of the Tamarit* proceeds from a remembrance of erotic attachment to a recognition of the fact of death, the element most frequently associated with lost love and portending death is water. The flow of water references through these poems calls to mind the Moorish civilization's sensual appreciation of water, which gave rise to so many fountains and channels both indoors and out. In "Gacela of the Dead Child" (*Gacela del niño muerto*), the poet tells us that a child dies every afternoon in Granada, and "every afternoon the water sits down / to converse with its friends"; he says further that "the day is a wounded boy." Perhaps this means that the child loses his innocence in the daytime of his life, so that the water must act as a purifying agent and take the child in a cleansing death; it was apparently in the fading afternoon that "you drowned in the river" and "your body, with the violet shadow of my hands / was—dead on the shore—an archangel of cold."

In "Gacela of the Dark Death" (*Gacela de la muerte oscura*), the poet seems to express an indifference toward physical death if only he can be remembered ("let everyone know that I have not died") or if he can retain consciousness (symbolized by Eden's fruit of knowledge, the apple):

Because I want to sleep the dream of apples
to learn a lament that will cleanse me of earth;
because I wish to live with that dark child
who wanted to cut out his own heart on the high sea.

*Porque quiero dormir el sueño de las manzanas*
*para aprender un llanto que me limpie de tierra;*
*porque quiero vivir con aquel niño oscuro*
*que quería cortarse el corazón en alta mar.*[44]

In "Casida of the Boy Wounded by Water" (*Casida del herido por el agua*), "pools, cisterns, and fountains / raise their swords in the air" in a fury of wounding love. The boy is clearly wounded by love as much as he is by water, but it is not clear whether the boy and the poet are the same person, for the poet wants to go down to the well as if to plumb the depths of his own suffering. There is a mirror effect in these lines along with their evocation of lacy Moorish vegetal patterns:

The boy and his agony, face to face,
were two intertwined green rains.
The boy was stretched on the ground
with his agony curving over him.

*El niño y su agonía, frente a frente,*
*eran dos verdes lluvias enlazadas,*
*El niño se tendía por la tierra*
*y su agonía se curvaba.*[45]

The poet says finally that he wants to die his own death in huge gulps, in order "to see the boy wounded by water." Recognition of the maturity with which Lorca faced his old fears and shames in these poems is the best preparation for examining his four last and greatest plays.

# 7

~·~·~·~·~·~·~·~·~·~·~·~·~·~·~·~·~·~·~·~·~·~·

# Theatre as Synthesis

Lorca's posthumous reputation as a dramatist has undergone several modifications in Spain from the period of controversy and confusion surrounding his assassination in 1936 to the present. The major changes in critical opinion prior to Franco's death in November 1975 are chronicled by Roberto G. Sánchez in "Lorca, the Post-War Theater and the Conflict of Generations,"[1] and Frank P. Casa comments on more recent reactions to Lorca in "Theatre after Franco: the First Reaction."[2] As noted in chapter 2 of this book, the publication of *The Audience* and *Play without a Title* will undoubtedly have an impact on critical interpretations of his other plays. In viewing Lorca's development as a progression toward a synthesis of all the arts, we see that an exclusionary interpretation of his work is not possible. Lorca was indeed becoming vitally concerned with social issues, but he never completely suppressed his poetic impulse. He was as conscious of universal truths as he was drawn to localized folkloric expression. He exulted in the stark realism he achieved in his last play, yet the visual design sensibility that informs that work is superbly stylized in its simplicity.

It is known that Lorca worked slowly, allowing his thoughts on a project to ripen before preparing a draft, polishing and correcting several drafts before releasing a work for publication or stage production. Lorca said that he spent five years on *Blood Wedding* and three years on *Yerma;*[3] he had begun thinking about *Doña Rosita the Spinster* as early as 1926.[4] Nevertheless —bearing in mind that Lorca had other, now lost, plays in progress at the time of his death—one can discern a trajectory of creative growth even within this final group of plays. The first, *Blood Wedding* (*Bodas de sangre,* 1933) corresponds in tone to the poems in *Deep Song* and *Gypsy Ballad;* it features musical passages, strong folkloric elements, and an abrupt stylistic shift into the haunting forest scene. The focus is narrowed in *Yerma* (1934) to concentrate on one woman's obsession, just as Lorca tightened up his field of vision in the short poems of *Songs* and *First Songs*. In *Doña Rosita the Spinster* (*Doña Rosita la soltera,* 1935), Lorca achieved his most complete synthesis of poetry, theatre, music, visual design, and popular arts. The play is at once a tragedy and a comedy; its action is poetic metaphor, but there is also some satirical social commentary. After such an apotheosis, the artist can only pull back in the direction of greater purity of form, just as Samuel Beckett has done in writing his plays with increasing economy of means. In Lorca's last play, *The House of Bernarda Alba* (*La Casa de Bernarda Alba,* 1936), the passions are the more intense because the plot, characterization, language, and theatrical elements are reduced to the bare essentials.

In 1935 and 1936, Lorca often spoke about the theatre in interviews and informal lectures. The philosophy he expressed on such occasions should be kept in mind as one analyzes the plays of this period. In his "Talk about the Theatre" (February 2, 1935), his idealism about a social function of theatre is evident:

The theatre is one of the most useful and expressive instruments for the edification of a country as well as the barometer that measures its greatness or decline. A theatre that is sensitive and properly oriented at all levels from tragedy to vaudeville can effect a change in people's outlook in just a few years, while a decadent theatre where hooves substitute for wings can cheapen an entire nation and put it to sleep. The theatre is a school of tears and laughter and a public forum where old and dubious morals can be put on trial and where living examples can be used to analyze eternal norms in the heart and mind of man. . . . Theatre must impose itself on the public and not the audience on the theatre.[5]

A 1935 interview with Nicolás González Deleito reveals Lorca's notion of an all-encompassing art of the theatre:

The problem of newness in the theatre is bound up to a great extent with the plastic arts. Half of the scenic effect depends upon rhythm, color, and scenography. . . . Every kind of theatre remains true to itself by capturing the rhythm of its own epoch, by integrating the emotions, sorrows, struggles, dramas of that epoch. . . . Theatre must encompass the total drama of present-day life. The theatre that has always endured is that of the poets. The theatre has always been in the hands of poets. And the greater the poet the better the theatre has been. That's not, of course, the lyrical poet, but the dramatic poet. . . . Dialogue in verse is not the same thing as poetry in the theatre. . . . There can be no theatre without poetic atmosphere, without inventiveness.[6]

Lorca's idea of a poetry of the theatre is further elaborated in an interview published in *La Voz* (Madrid, April 7, 1936):

Theatre has always been my vocation. I have given many hours of my life to the theatre. I have a firm, personal concept of a certain kind of theatre. Theatre is poetry that rises from the page and becomes human. And in so doing, it speaks and cries out, weeps and despairs. The theatre requires that the characters appearing on stage wear a cloak of poetry and at the same time allow us to see their flesh and blood.[7]

In his last published interview (*El Sol*, Madrid, June 10, 1936), Lorca left no doubt of his concern that poetry be reconciled with reality:

No true man still believes in that rubbish about pure art, art for art's sake. At this dramatic moment in the course of world events, the artist must weep and laugh with his own people. He must put aside the spray of lilies and wade waist-deep into the mud to help those who are looking for lilies. Personally, I am most anxious to communicate with others. That's why I have come calling at the doors of the theatre, and to the theatre I consecrate all my sensibilities.[8]

Critics often refer to *Blood Wedding, Yerma,* and *The House of Bernarda Alba* as a trilogy.[9] Although the stories of the three tragedies are unrelated, all are set in rural Andalusia and focus on women in relation to problems of marriage, passionate impulses, and death. Francesca Colecchia says that these plays share a concern for "the pervasive role of religion in Spanish life" and for the inescapable impact that it has on the everyday lives of the people.[10] Religious and societal constraints on these women's lives are treated metaphorically in the plays, as discussed in Harriet S. Turner's article on "Circularity and Closure in Lorca's trilogy."[11]

*Blood Wedding* begins with an exchange between the Mother and her grown son, who is designated only as the Bridegroom. The Mother is a character of considerable presence who dominates her son, the only man in her household. Her husband died of a knife wound after only three years of marriage, and, later, their first son was also killed in her family's continuing feud with the Felix family. Now the Mother's entire purpose in life is to protect her only remaining child. She hesitates to give him the knife he needs to work in the vineyard, tries to prevent him from going out of the house, and even tells him she wishes he were a woman. The intensity of her desire to restrict—in effect, to emasculate—her son conflicts with her hopes for fertility: she reproaches him for neglecting the land near the mill (although he has worked hard to buy the vineyard that he now hopes to use as a bargaining chip in winning the

girl he has been courting for three years). In consenting to go to the Bride's house to arrange the marriage, the Mother expresses a wish for grandchildren, especially girls, who will stay peacefully at home embroidering with her. Yet she says wistfully: "Your grandfather left a son on every corner. I like that. Men, men; wheat, wheat."

After the Bridegroom goes out, a Neighbor stops in to visit. She reports that a neighbor's son lost both arms, cut off by a machine; her statement recalls the severed limbs often mentioned in Lorca's poetry or seen in his drawings, and it serves as a reminder of sudden, unforeseeable dangers in life. Since the nature of the machine is unspecified, that mention may provoke a thought about the meaning of the industrial age in a rural village. The Mother and the Neighbor discuss the Bride, who lives with her Father ten leagues from the nearest house. When she was fifteen or so, the Bride had a sweetheart, but that man has been married for two years to the Bride's cousin. The Mother learns the man's name: Leonardo Felix. It is significant that he is the only character in the play given an individual name; the names of the others suggest that they are archetypal figures.

Scene 2 opens with a lullaby sung by Leonardo's Wife and Mother-in-Law to the baby. It is a disturbing song about a big horse who didn't like water, but died, bleeding in the stream. (In his lecture "On Lullabies," Lorca discussed at length the characteristic violence and cruelty of Spanish cradle songs.) When Leonardo enters, he quickly becomes associated with the horse, just as the Bridegroom's symbol is the phallic knife. The horse is a symbol of masculinity, and the refusal of the horse in the song to drink from the stream might refer to Leonardo's rebellion against family values. Leonardo lies to his Wife about his hard use of the horse; he had been seen riding in the arid territory where his

Wife's cousin lives. A little girl comes to tell them about the expensive presents the Bridegroom has bought for the Bride. Leonardo becomes angry and stalks out.

The visit of the Mother and the Bridegroom to the Bride's house is a formal and stilted-sounding sequence. With the Bride's Father, they discuss the wasteland on which the Father has labored to get a satisfactory harvest of hemp. The lack of water on his land implies metaphorically that this is not fertile ground for a marriage. The distance of his lands from the Bridegroom's vineyards will mean extra work for the Bridegroom; he will clearly have to work hard also to achieve a meaningful union with the Bride. They decide that the wedding will be the next Thursday, and then they summon the Bride into the room. She enters modestly, her head bowed. The Mother tells her what it is to be married: "A man, some children, and a wall six feet thick for all else."

As soon as the Father leads the Mother and Bridegroom out, the Bride releases her pent-up emotion in a show of anger, grabbing her Servant's wrists. The Servant exclaims: "You are stronger than a man," and the Bride replies: "Haven't I worked like a man? I wish I were one!" This is the second expression of a desire for a change of sex in the play. A reading of Lorca's 1930 play, *The Audience*, throws such lines into greater relief. The Servant then tells the Bride that she heard a horse last night and was shocked to see its rider—Leonardo—at the Bride's window. Just then the sound of a horse is heard outside. The Servant rushes to the window and sees Leonardo galloping away.

Act 2 takes place on the wedding day. While combing the Bride's hair before dawn, the Servant is horrified at the quick-tempered Bride's flinging away of the wreath of orange blossoms, an act which the Servant sees as a bad omen. The first guest to arrive is

Leonardo, who came on his horse while his Wife travels by the road in a cart. Still wearing only her petticoats, the Bride confronts him. They argue about his marriage to her cousin. Leonardo claims that the Bride forced him to marry another, apparently because she didn't want to live in poverty, but he tells her that when something burns so deeply inside one, nobody can uproot it. The Bride begins to fall under his spell, but checks herself when a chorus of wedding guests is heard singing a traditional song to the Bride as they approach the house. She rushes out of the room, repeating a line from the song: "Wake up the Bride!" Although she will struggle desperately to keep her troth to the Bridegroom, she is awakening to the realization that the marriage will be a frustrating trap for her.

The wedding party's entrance is a colorful procession with singing and guitar accompaniment. The Bride re-enters, dressed for the wedding, and urges the Bridegroom to get her to the church quickly, so that she will hear no voice but his and see no eyes but his. The scene ends with a brief exchange between Leonardo and his Wife. She asks him why he looks at her "with a thorn in each eye." She knows that she no longer means anything to him, but at least she has given birth to his son, and another is on the way. They leave together for the church.

It is late afternoon when the wedding party returns from the church to the Bride's home. Although the Bride's Father tries to keep the mood cheerful, the Mother is upset at seeing members of the Felix family among the wedding guests, and she broods about her dead. The guests mill around, while Leonardo lurks in the background. Two girls argue over who received the first pin from the Bride, since according to folk superstition that would guarantee marriage. The Bride speaks curtly to them, irritated by their eagerness to marry. The Bridegroom tries to embrace her, but she says she needs to rest a little. After she goes out, the Mother advises her son—the way his father would, if he were alive—on how to handle a wife and make her realize that he is "the man, the boss, the one who gives the orders."

Leonardo's Wife rushes in with the news that she saw the Bride and Leonardo ride away together on his horse. The Mother immediately calls for a horse so that her son can go after them: the girl may be shameless, but she is now the Bridegroom's Wife, so the Mother's family honor is at stake. Upon second thought, the Mother remembers the danger to her son, but she conquers her fears and sends him off. Suddenly, the wedding celebrants are divided into two opposing groups. The Mother shouts "After them! after them!" as the act ends.

The first scene of Act 3 is stylistically distinct from the rest of the play. It is set in a dark forest, its unreal atmosphere enhanced by the sound of violins. Three Woodcutters discuss the runaway couple; they speculate that by now he must be loving her. The Moon, portrayed as a young woodcutter with a white face, enters, flooding the stage with radiant blue light. His poetic incantation reinforces the ominousness of the scene: his rays are a knife abandoned in the air, rays that seek the warmth inside a breast, rays that must get in everywhere among the branches and leave no shadow to hide the lovers. The Moon will cooperate with Death, who enters in the guise of an Old Beggar Woman, sits, and covers herself with a cloak.

The Bridegroom on the trail of the lovers enters and stumbles into the Beggar Woman. The Bridegroom does not understand the woman's meaning when she says that he would be handsomer if he were asleep, laid out on his back; he accepts her offer to guide him. Together they exit.

In a sensual and poetic sequence between Leonardo and the Bride, she tries to renounce him, but he reminds her that it was she who bridled his horse and put spurs on him. They embrace and realize that they cannot give each other up. They exit, resolved to face death together. A stage direction indicates how the forest scene is to end:

The Moon enters very slowly. The stage is bathed in a strong blue light. The two violins are heard. Suddenly two long ear-splitting screams are heard, cutting off the violin music. On the second scream the Old Beggar Woman appears and stands with her back to the audience. She opens her cape and remains at center, like a great bird with immense wings. The Moon stops. The curtain comes down in complete silence.[12]

The final scene is a coda that brings together all the women of the play in a stark white room apparently in the Mother's house, although Lorca specifies that it must have "the monumental feeling of a church. There must be no hint of gray, nor any shadow, not even anything to suggest perspective." Against that whiteness, the skein of red wool that two girls are winding serves as an objective correlative for their song about the thread of life; that is, the red wool seems to supply the word "blood," which never occurs in the song.

Leonardo's Mother-in-Law tells Leonardo's Wife that she must now grow old alone, sequestered in her house, with "a cross of ashes on the bed where his pillow was." The Old Beggar Woman appears in the doorway and speaks pleasurably of the two deaths:

Broken blossoms their eyes, and their teeth
two handfuls of hardened snow.
Both of them fell, and the bride returns,
her skirt and hair stained with blood.
They come covered with two cloths,
carried on the shoulders of tall youths.

*Flores rotas los ojos, y sus dientes*
*dos puñados de nieve endurecida.*

*Los dos cayeron, y la novia vuelve*
*teñida en sangre falde y cabellera.*
*Cubiertos con dos mantas ellos vienen*
*sobre los hombros de los mozos altos.*[13]

Finally, the Mother enters, accompanied by her Neighbor, who is weeping. The Mother cannot shed mere tears from her eyes, but says that her tears will come from the soles of her feet, from her roots, and they will burn more than blood. She will live in peace at last, having nothing more to fear of guns and knives; nothing more can be taken from her.

The Bride enters and allows the Mother to beat her in hopes that she will be killed and carried away with the two men. She insists, however, that she is still a virgin and that she did not want to betray the Bridegroom: she was a woman on fire and the Bridegroom was "a trickle of water from which I hoped for children, land, health; but the other was a dark river full of branches . . . who dragged me like the pull of the sea, like the butting of a mule, and would have dragged me always, always, always. . . ." The Mother allows the Bride to join in her lamentation, but only from the doorway. Several neighbors enter, kneel, and sob while the Mother laments. It would be difficult to better the Graham-Luján and O'Connell translation of this particular passage:

> With a knife,
> with a tiny knife
> that barely fits the hand,
> but that slides in clean
> through the astonished flesh
> and stops at the place
> where trembles, enmeshed,
> the dark root of a scream.[14]

> *Con un cuchillo,*
> *con un cuchillito*
> *que apenas cabe en la mano,*

> *pero que penetra fino*
> *por las carnes asombradas*
> *y que se para en el sitio*
> *donde tiembla enmarañada*
> *la oscura raíz del grito.*[15]

*Blood Wedding* has often been compared to John Millington Synge's *Riders to the Sea* (1904), since that one-act Irish folk tragedy contains a similar mix of peasant superstition and religion; there is the same sense of unavoidable destiny among the two peoples whose lives depend so closely on their geographical environment. Certainly, the outward stoicism of the Mother in Lorca's coda is comparable to the behavior of Maurya in the final tableau of Synge's play: her neighbors keen while Maurya sits calmly because she now has no son left to lose.

*Blood Wedding* is an excellent example of Lorca's ability to fuse poetry and reality, for it was based on a short account Lorca had read in a Granada newspaper of a bride from Almería who ran off with another man on her wedding day, followed by the bridegroom who killed and was killed by the seducer.[16] The visual artist's sensibilities are evident in the precise specifications of color for the settings, costumes, lighting, and props. The contrast in rhythm and mood between the buoyant chaos of the guests dancing at the wedding festivities and the slow, deliberate incantations in the eerie nocturnal forest is a highly theatrical effect. Although *Blood Wedding* is generally ranked beneath *The House of Bernarda Alba* as an artistic achievement, it is the most frequently performed of Lorca's plays in the United States.[17]

*Yerma* is less frequently staged than the other two tragedies, but it has generated the most critical commentary. Despite its narrow focus, *Yerma* is an amazingly rich and complex play that supports endless discussion of such questions as: who is to blame for

Yerma's barrenness? is the crucial theme of the play
maternal instinct or is it about honor? or is the play really about the failure of religion? how does the poetic
imagery affect our perceptions of the characters? is the
fertility rite on the mountain an actual event or is it
Yerma's hallucination? is Yerma a tragic heroine?

Lorca subtitled *Yerma* "A Tragic Poem in Three
Acts and Six Scenes." The action spans a period of
about three years, beginning in the second year of
Yerma's childless marriage to Juan. The first scene suggests what those first two years have been like: Yerma
is solicitous of Juan's welfare; he is secure in the knowledge that she loves him. It is apparent that she has
hinted to him before of her desire for children, but that
desire has not yet become a source of contention between them. The play's action begins at the point when
Yerma is beginning to find it difficult to hide her longing. It is significant that the play opens with a dream
sequence. Yerma lies asleep and in "a strange dream-
light" a Shepherd enters on tiptoe, leading by the hand
a Child dressed in white. The Shepherd and the Child
disappear when the clock strikes; morning sunlight fills
the stage, and Yerma awakens. Thus have her desires
hitherto been interiorized. The dream sequence also
points up subsequent scattered references to Yerma's
active imagination (as in Scene 2, when she is talking
with Victor and she thinks she hears a child crying as if
it were drowning). The fact that she dreams of a Shepherd bringing her a child may hint at her subconscious
attraction to the shepherd Victor, or it may refer to
Christ the Good Shepherd. The latter interpretation is
proposed in Dennis Klein's useful article, "Christological Imagery in Lorca's *Yerma*."[18]

The subjectivity of that opening sequence suggests
that the events and characters in the play are perhaps
filtered through Yerma's perceptions. She is present on
stage at virtually every moment of the play except dur-

ing the two "choral interludes." The monotony of her
long wait for fulfillment is suggested in the structural
division of the play into three acts of two scenes each,
the first scene in each act occurring in the early morning, the second scene at twilight, a visual poetry of regularly repeated brightening and dimming of the stage.
Furthermore, Lorca's deliberate ambiguity in his han-
dling of the reasons for Yerma's barrenness is a reflection of Yerma's ingenuousness: like most Spanish young
women, she knows little about what it takes to make a
baby and, thus inadequately informed, is susceptible to
folk remedies and superstitions.

After awakening from her dream, Yerma sees Juan
off to his work in the fields. Lorca specifies that she
takes the initiative in kissing Juan; it is important to establish the good will with which she entered into marriage and tried to make it work. When Juan has left,
Yerma sits down to her sewing; her song is an imaginary dialogue she carries on with her wished-for child.
She is visited by her younger friend Maria, who has
been married only five months and is already with
child. Maria is not certain what caused her condition: it
seems to her that her child is a dove of light that her
husband slipped into her ear. She is well aware that she
knows nothing about such things, but says: "I'll ask my
mother what I must do." Yerma is moved by Maria's
pregnancy and reveals—perhaps for the first time to
someone other than her husband—the extent of her
own longing. She goes so far as to say: "If I continue
this way, I'll end up by turning bad." When Victor
stops in a few moments later, he is quite unaware of
having touched a raw nerve when he tells Yerma that
her house needs a child in it. After he leaves, Yerma
"crosses to the place where Victor stood and breathes
deeply, as if inhaling mountain air."

A year later, Yerma is just returning from taking
dinner to her husband in the olive grove when she

meets an Old Woman who has nine children. Yerma is eager to talk to an older woman who might explain certain things to her, but the Old Woman raises more questions than she answers: Hasn't Yerma's husband ever made her tremble when he comes near? Yerma replies that only Victor once made her feel like that, but when her father chose Juan she married him happily, anticipating children. Now she is "filling up with hate." Yerma's openness about her preoccupations shows how much she has changed in a year, the third year of her marriage.

Yerma then meets two Girls, one of whom mentions that her mother has certain methods of helping women who want children. Yerma asks: "Doesn't your mother live in the farthest up house in the village?" Yerma will finally get to that house in Act 3, Scene 1, and her quest will culminate in the final scene up on a mountainside. That upward movement might reflect either her psychological uphill battle or her Golgotha-like ascent toward an inverted kind of redemption.

Yerma's encounter with Victor, in which she imagines that she hears a child crying, is interrupted by the appearance of Juan, who reproaches her for not having hurried directly home so that people won't talk about her. When Juan speaks of behavior that is becoming in a woman, she replies: "I wish I were a woman."

The village women who wash their clothes in a stream in Act 2, Scene 1, have been compared to a chorus in classical Greek tragedy. They are situated on several levels to create a formal stage picture. The scene begins and ends with their rhythmic singing, but the central sequence is gossip about Yerma, who does not appear. We learn that Juan has brought his two old-maid sisters to live in his house and keep an eye on Yerma. One of the washerwomen insinuates that Yerma has another man on her mind. There is some argument over whether her failure to have children is her fault or his. Yerma's sisters-in-law enter and begin to do their washing. The song is resumed, full of water and floral imagery, celebrating both cleanliness and fecundity.

The next scene occurs at twilight in Juan and Yerma's house, in the fifth year of their marriage. Juan has worked so hard pruning apple trees that he is too tired to lift an apple to his mouth. Since Lorca often used the apple to symbolize reasoned awareness, it is not surprising when we see how unreasonable Juan has become about Yerma's leaving the house: he even resents her having gone to the fountain for fresh water for his dinner. Juan's sisters come and go throughout the altercation between husband and wife. Juan has lost patience with Yerma's obsession, but he suggests that she bring one of her brother's children to live with them. He tells her that she is "not a real woman," and she replies: "I don't know what I am." He orders her not to talk to anyone outside the house, then goes in to eat in the other room with his sisters.

From her doorway, Yerma calls to Maria to bring her child in. In contrast to her previous scene with Maria, Yerma now compulsively talks about the hurt she feels. She sees signs of fertility everywhere around the village, while she feels that she is losing her femininity, becoming quite mannish. She refers to the uselessness of her hands, a foreshadowing of the destruction her hands will wreak in the last scene of the play. This reference also points up the extent to which she has changed in the course of the play, since she had once been considered an exceptionally good seamstress.

Victor stops in to say goodbye; his family is moving away. After their reticent leavetaking with its undercurrent of torment, Yerma slips off with the Girl whose mother, Dolores, has been very successful at inducing pregnancy in women who want children.

Act 3, Scene 1 is set in Dolores's house at daybreak. Yerma, acting under Dolores's guidance, has spent the night praying in the cemetery. She is now more eager than ever to talk about personal matters. She knows that her husband is a good man, but she no longer loves him. She would like to have children by herself, but since she knows that they are born of man and woman together, her husband is her only salvation, her only honorable way to motherhood. Juan and his two sisters arrive, having tracked down Yerma. Juan's only concern seems to be that her conduct will provoke gossip that will sully his honor. Yerma defends her own family's honor, which she would never do anything to compromise. Critics who, like Robert Skloot,[19] base their interpretation of the play upon the question of honor need to make the distinction between Juan's concept of honor as social reputation and Yerma's notion of inner purity.

Yerma makes a final plea for some basis of understanding between her and her husband:

YERMA *(in an outburst, embracing her husband):* I'm looking for you. I'm looking for you. It's you I look for day and night without finding a resting place. It's your blood and your refuge I want.

JUAN: Get away from me.

YERMA: Don't push me aside if you want me.

JUAN: Leave me alone!

YERMA: Look how I am left alone. As if the moon were looking for herself in the sky. Look at me![20]

He pushes her away, she cries out, and he tells her to be quiet or people will hear her. She continues to shout, saying that her voice is her last remaining freedom. Dolores joins in with Juan's plea for silence. For a tragic heroine, Yerma comes perilously close to insanity at this point. She speaks almost incessantly of her hands, her head, her body, and finally her mouth, which she resolves shall henceforth be mute.

The final scene is set at a hermitage in the mountains where childless women make a pilgrimage every year. According to the Old Woman, the annual pilgrim-

age has begun to attract single men who are ready to
take advantage of the barren wives. Maria has accompanied Yerma, who had refused for the past month to
leave her chair. As night falls, Yerma and six other
women enter, barefoot, carrying candles. They sing a
joyous and hopeful song of fertility. A procession passes, bearing aloft two huge folk masks, one Male and
one Female. The Masks' poetic incantations are accompanied by dancing and the sound of bells and guitars.
The Old Woman draws Yerma aside and proposes that
she come to live in her house, since her son needs a
woman; she and her son would see that Yerma's husband was kept away and they would simply not worry
about gossip. Yerma does not even stop to consider
such a solution. Angry at being rebuffed, the Old
Woman calls Yerma *marchita*, which is almost synony-
mous with her name, *yerma*, meaning "barren." Yerma
says that she has been turning from that word, but now
that someone has said it to her face, she fears it is true.

When the Old Woman leaves, Juan comes out. He
had been eavesdropping, but he is not consoled by the
proof he has overheard of Yerma's honor. He is no
longer willing to put up with her continual lamentation
over something that simply does not matter to him:
"What matters to me is what I hold in my hands. What
I see with my eyes. . . . I am happy without children.
Neither of us is to blame." He finds her beautiful in the
moonlight and embraces her, but she sees that his desire for her is a mere physical appetite: "You want me
the way you might want pigeon to eat." She grasps him
by the throat and strangles him. The chorus of the pilgrimage is heard. He dies and Yerma realizes that she
has killed her only hope for a child. People begin to
gather around her, but she is now completely alone in
her barrenness. Yerma's tragedy, like that of the
Mother in *Blood Wedding*, is to have to go on living a
life without hope.

The heroine of *Doña Rosita the Spinster* is also ultimately condemned to a hopeless existence, with the difference that she struggles against even acknowledging the hopelessness of her situation. Although the play is not usually considered a tragedy, Rosita attains a tragic sublimity within the ridiculously pathetic role that life forces upon her. In 1934 Lorca called this play a comedy, describing the work-in-progress to an interviewer as "a piece of gentle ironies, of compassionate strokes of caricature; bourgeois comedy with mild tones and, diluted in it, the charm and delicacies of bygone days and different ways."[21] There is, indeed, much comedy in the play, but—as Lorca implied in a 1935 interview—it also contains elements of tragedy and social commentary: "It deals with the tragic current in the life of our society: Spanish women who remain unmarried. . . . I harvest the tragedy of cheap affectation in provincial Spain, something that will provoke laughter in the young generation, but whose dramatic effect has deep social importance, because it reflects what the middle class was."[22] The title and subtitle under which the play was published reflect the difficulty of confining it to a single genre: *Doña Rosita the Spinster; or The Language of the Flowers*; "A Poem of Granada in the 1900s, Divided into Several Gardens with Scenes of Singing and Dancing."

Besides embracing comfortably several literary genres, *Doña Rosita the Spinster* is Lorca's finest achievement of a synthesis of music, visual design, and folk entertainment in one wholly theatrical work. Visual elements enhance or comment ironically upon the ideas in the play. The changes in Rosita, for example, find their objective correlative not only in the *rosa mutabile*, but also in her costumes, in the setting, in the props she uses, and in the kinds of people from outside the household who call upon her. Other things, by contrast, never change, such as the tone, rhythm, and scope of variations in the arguments between the Aunt and the Housekeeper. The local color is of the city Lorca knew best, the "enclosed garden" of Granada.

It is possible that *Doña Rosita the Spinster* was Lorca's favorite of his own plays. It was the one—he said in 1934—into which he was putting all his enthusiasm,[23] and—he said later—the one into which he had put the most important of his deeply felt convictions.[24] In any case, it was the play about which are recorded the greatest number of comments by Lorca. His *précis* of the play on the occasion of its opening in Barcelona on December 13, 1935, is worth reproducing at length:

*Doña Rosita* is the outwardly gentle but inwardly parched life of a Granadan maiden, who little by little gets transformed into the grotesque and touching thing that is a spinster in Spain. Each act of the work takes place in a different period. The first occurs in the starched and prim years around 1885. Bustle, elaborate hairstyle, lots of wool and silk to cover the flesh, colored parasols. . . . Doña Rosita is twenty then. She is full of hope. The second act is set in 1900. Wasp waists, bellflower-shaped skirts, the Paris Exposition, modernism, the first automobiles. . . . Doña Rosita reaches full physical maturity. It grieves me a bit to have to say that a touch of lassitude begins to appear among her charms. Third act: 1911. Hobble skirt, aeroplanes. One step further, war. One might say that the basic upheavals that produce a world conflagration are already present in souls and objects. In this act Doña Rosita is already nearly half a century old. Withered bosom, narrow hips, eyes with a faraway look, ashes in her mouth and in her unbecomingly arranged braids. . . . On the posters I call this play a poem for families, and that's exactly what it is. How many mature Spanish women will see themselves reflected in Doña Rosita as in a mirror! I wanted to follow the purest possible line from beginning to end of this comedy. Did I call it a comedy? It's better to say the drama of Spanish tastelessness, of Spanish hypocrisy, and of our women's need to repress by force into the depths of their blighted dispositions any desire for personal pleasure.[25]

It is unfortunate that *Doña Rosita the Spinster* has tended to be neglected in the American theatre, its au-

thorized English version overshadowed perhaps by the
better translations available for the "tragic trilogy." Few
plays in the world evoke a way of life with so much nostalgia and cruelty combined in one work of such consummate stylistic grace. Its three-act structure and its
dominant symbol reinforce the changes that occur
in the protagonist's development from the red morning through the coral noon to the colorless evening of
her life.

The play is set in the house of the doting Uncle
and Aunt who—together with their earthy, outspoken
Housekeeper—have raised the orphan Rosita from
childhood. The Uncle is a botanist, and his obsession
with flowers of all kinds is the motivational basis for the
play's texture, imagery, symbolism. In Act 1 he has just
succeeded in growing in his greenhouse a *rosa mutabile*, a rare species that completes its entire life cycle
with striking changes of color in a single day's time. Its
description is read in full or in part several times during
the play from a book about roses:

> In the morning it opens
> red as blood,
> untouched by dew that fears
> to be burned.
> Full-blown at noon, it is
> hard as coral.
> The sun beats on the windows
> to see it glow.
> When the birds in the branches
> begin to sing
> and the afternoon faints
> on the seas' violets,
> it turns white, to the whiteness
> of a cheek of salt.
> And when night sounds flat notes
> on its metal horn
> while the stars advance
> and breezes stall,

on the threshhold of darkness
its petals fall.

*Cuando se abre la mañana,*
*roja como sangre está.*
*El rocío no toca*
*porque se teme quemar.*
*Abierta en el mediodía*
*es dura como el coral.*
*El sol se asoma a los vidrios*
*para verla relumbrar.*
*Cuando en las ramas empiezan*
*los pájaros a cantar*
*y se desmaya la tarde*
*en las violetas del mar,*
*se pone blanca, con blanco*
*de una mejilla de sal.*
*Y cuando toca la noche*
*blando cuerno de metal*
*y las estrellas avanzan*
*mientras los aires se van,*
*en la raya de lo oscuro,*
*se comienza a deshojar.*[26]

Rosita dashes in and out collecting her hat and parasol
for an outing with her friends, the Manolas. The
Housekeeper constantly interposes her folk superstitions, and she delights in scandalizing the Aunt with
whispered indecencies from peasant lore. The two
women, who function equally as surrogate mothers of
Rosita, can scarcely be in the same room together without attempting to manipulate each other emotionally.
Although their formal relationship is one of servant to
mistress, and although the servant usually comes out on
top in their wryly humorous encounters, there is a deep
unspoken bond of affection between them.

Rosita is engaged to her handsome cousin, the
Nephew of the Aunt and Uncle. He pays a call while
Rosita is out and tells the Aunt that he has received a
letter from his parents in Tucumán, a forty-day journey

across the Atlantic, summoning him to join them there to help out on the plantation. He would like to marry Rosita now and take her with him, but the Aunt—concerned for her family's social image—insists that he first become self-supporting. The Housekeeper, who had been eavesdropping, bursts into the room in tears; she is against the Aunt's decision. The Nephew departs hastily while the Housekeeper recites a folk charm and makes a cross on the floor with water as an expression of her concern for Rosita.

Rosita returns with the three Manolas, young and pretty coquettes who swirl into the room as they close their parasols and sing of their romantic longings and of Granada in the jasmine-perfumed moonlight. Rosita joins in the song which evokes Granada by naming specific streets and landmarks. The Housekeeper sends Rosita to talk with her Aunt and hurries the Manolas on their way. While the stage is left momentarily empty, a distant piano is heard playing a Czerny étude. This is a particularly Chekhovian touch in a play that critics often compare to the best works of Anton Chekhov.

Rosita and the Nephew appear almost simultaneously in the doorways on opposite sides of the room. The emotion of the moment is perfectly expressed in the visual stage picture. They look at each other, then come together, his arm around her waist, her head on his shoulder. When they finally speak, it is the play's only poetic dialogue passage that is not part of a song. The exchange of promises and tender farewells abounds redolently with flower imagery. Three times he swears he will return. After he leaves, Rosita, weeping, picks up the book of roses and reads the poem of the *rosa mutabile*.

Act 2 takes place on Rosita's saint's day in 1900. Mr. X, a professor of Political Economy, has come to call on her, but has ended up in conversation with the Uncle. They discuss the outlook for the new century.

Mr. X is thrilled with the latest technological marvels despite the destructiveness of some of them, while the Uncle, convinced that it will be "a materialistic century," is content to immerse himself quietly in his botanical studies; in their opposite extremes of attitude both men appear ridiculous. Mr. X leaves a gift for Rosita: a pendant with a "mother-of-pearl Eiffel Tower over two doves that carry the wheel of industry in their beaks." He chose it as more tasteful than the "little silver cannon with a view through its mouth of the Virgin of Lourdes" that he also considered. Lorca's mockery of aesthetic vulgarity does not exempt the peasant class, since the Housekeeper's gift for Rosita is a "Louis XV-style thermometer holder," in which the thermometer figures as a stream of water in a miniature scene made of shells, sequins, paint, and gold thread on a velvet backing.

The Housekeeper claims credit for getting Mr. X to leave by applying one of her folk charms: she put a broom upside down behind the door. She is disgusted that such men present themselves as suitors to Rosita. It is fifteen years since the Nephew left, and the cupboards are bulging with an accumulation of linens that Rosita has been embroidering over the years in preparation for her marriage. The materialistic impulse that produces this trousseau under the encouragement of the Uncle and Aunt is not fully evident until Act 3, when they realize too late that the amassed goods cannot compensate for a missing dimension in their emotional lives.

When the Aunt wants to cut some of the Uncle's roses for the vase in the entrance hall, he protests that he cannot bear to see his roses cut off and stuck in vases. The irony of his comment is that the family's pretensions have cut Rosita off from life and left her stranded in the house like a rose in a vase. The Aunt advises Rosita to break off with the Nephew who has been away so long and to marry one of the many youths or mature men who are in love with her. Rosita replies: "But Aunt! I have deep roots, deeply buried in my feelings. If I didn't see other people I could believe that he left only a week ago. I wait as if it were the first day. Besides, what is a year, or two, or five?"

Two groups of callers arrive to pay their respects to Rosita on her saint's day. The first is a Mother with her three Spinster daughters, all dressed in cheap, flashy clothes; their manners are equally vulgar: they give Rosita a tacky paper barometer with a bit of doggerel on it and then the Mother launches into a tirade about her financial difficulties. They hint for refreshments, although the Mother boasts that whenever she gives her daughters a choice of eggs for breakfast or chairs at the promenade, they unhesitatingly choose the chairs. Her little story must have gained wide currency, for when the two Ayola young ladies arrive a bit later, one of them cruelly mocks the Spinsters, saying as she refuses refreshments, "We ate just a little while ago. I confess I ate four eggs with tomato sauce and could hardly get up from my chair." Rosita tries to shield the Spinsters from the rudeness of the young, insensitive Ayolas. She is metaphorically caught in the middle, no longer girlish like the Ayolas, but not yet a spinster since she is engaged. The first Ayola goes so far as to say: "If I'm Rosita's friend, it's because she has a fiancé. Women who don't have a boyfriend are faded and warmed-over . . . ." The Spinsters offer their hosts some parlor entertainment: the Third Spinster plays the piano while the others sing "The Language of the Flowers."

The mailman brings a letter for Rosita from the Nephew: he wants to marry her, but since he cannot yet get away he proposes a marriage by proxy. Everyone rejoices at this except the Housekeeper, to whom it is explained that someone represents the groom in the ceremony and then Rosita will be a married woman.

The Housekeeper's down-to-earth response is: "And
what happens at night? . . . Let him come in person
and get married! . . . Mistress, I don't think much of
those proxies!" The Uncle enters, carrying a rose, and
says that he overheard everything and in his excitement
he cut the only *rosa mutabile* in his greenhouse while it
was still red: if he had delayed cutting it only two hours
more he could have given it to Rosita in its last—white
—phase. In her article on "Time, Irony, and Negation
in Lorca's Last Three Plays," Kathleen Dolan offers a
clear explanation of the analogy that Lorca intended
here: "Rosita's mutation from ingenue to *solterona* is
halted by the letter with its false promise, and her illu-
sion, coinciding with the 'noon' of her existence, is symbolically crystallized in the image of the cut rose."[27]
With all the dramatic focus on the rose that the Uncle
gives to Rosita, she softly speaks some haunting lines
from the poem of Act 1. The quiet intensity of that moment in the action is broken when the Spinster at the
piano begins to play a polka. All join in a lively dance;
Rosita's partnering of one of the Spinsters again fore-
shadows her fate.

Act 3 takes place in the evening. The deterioration
of the house testifies to the passage of ten more years.
The Uncle died six years earlier and now the women
must move to a smaller place. The Aunt has learned
only recently that the Nephew has been married for
eight years to a wealthy woman in Tucumán. In her
helpless rage over Rosita's having been strung along until it is too late for her to get a husband, the Housekeeper suggests sending the Nephew a poisoned letter
so that he would die instantly upon receiving it. It is a
humorous line of dialogue, but it can also be read in the
context of Lorca's comment on the small precedents in
individual lives for evil turns of event in world history.

They receive a visitor, Don Martín, a sad-looking
old man with red hair and a crutch, apparently modeled

on one of Lorca's former teachers at the Colegio del
Sagrado Corazón. He speaks of the difficulties of trying
to teach the spoiled children of rich parents. He always
dreamed of being a poet and even wrote a drama that
never got produced. Its title, *The Daughter of Jephté*,
is the same as that of the unproduced opera written by
Lorca's beloved music teacher, Don Antonio Segura.
The Aunt reminds Don Martín that he already lent
them his play, which she and Rosita had read four or
five times. He cadges compliments and recites some of
the work's pompously rhetorical verse. Lorca's mature
skill in balancing one theatrical moment against another
is superbly exemplified by the pathetic old man's decla-
mation of overblown tragic sentiments, followed immediately by the entrance of two Workmen who pick up a
large sofa and carry it out slowly as if it were a coffin,
while a church bell tolls the half hour. Suddenly Don
Martín is summoned to the school: the children have
broken some pipes and the classrooms are flooded.
Again, Lorca is clearly presaging the chaos of World
War I. Don Martín exits, saying "I dreamed of Parnas-
sus and I end up being a mason and a plumber."

Rosita enters, wearing a pale rose-tinted dress and
holding a packet of letters. The prop has no function in
the ensuing scene, but serves to signal to the audience
that she still carries the Nephew's words in her heart.
She is glad that they will be leaving the house after
dark, because she cannot bear being pointed out as an
old maid by children in the street and it wounds her
pride to think that the neighbors will talk about their
fall into ruin. She knows that they have lost their house
only because the Uncle mortgaged it to pay for her
now-useless bridal trousseau. She doesn't want to talk
about that illusory wedding, but the Aunt insists:
"That's what's wrong with decent women from around
here. Not speaking! We don't speak, but we have got to
speak." Rosita then reveals that she has known all along

that the Nephew had married: a charitable soul had
taken the trouble to inform her. She was willing to go
on believing the lies in his letters, but others would not
even allow her that comfort, because "everyone knew
and I found myself pointed out by a finger that made
my engaged girl's modesty seem ridiculous and gave
my maiden's fan a grotesque quality." Rosita's long
speech is a beautifully written, heart-rending mono-
logue; it builds to an admission of intellectual awareness
of the death of hope, although emotionally "hope pur-
sues me, hounds me, nips at me, like a dying wolf
clenching its teeth for the last time."

As the women prepare to leave the house, an eighteen-year-old Youth looks in, surprised to see that they
are moving. He is the son of the oldest of the three
Manolas, and his brief but poignant appearance illustrates Rosita's observation that "there is nothing more
alive than a memory." Rosita puts on a long white coat
over her dress. As night falls, it begins to rain. Rosita's
final words on stage are the last two lines of the poem:
"on the threshhold of darkness / its petals fall." They
exit and the stage is left empty. The greenhouse door,
swollen with dampness so that it cannot be closed,
is heard banging. "Suddenly a French window in the
upstage wall flies open and white curtains flutter in
the wind."

That final stage direction is but one example of
Lorca's mastery of a language of the stage quite apart
from dialogue. The combination of the sound effect and
the visual image—the inspiration of Lorca as musician
and painter—reinforces the actors' art in illuminating
for a theatre audience what it means to be human, and
exemplifies to perfection what Cocteau and other
French theorists have called a "poetry of the theatre,"
rather than mere poetry in the theatre.

Having perfected in *Doña Rosita the Spinster* his
ability to synthesize several arts within a theatrical

form, Lorca could then proceed to stretch the formal possibilities of the theatre in other ways. There are only two extant examples known to date of works for the theatre written by Lorca after *Doña Rosita the Spinster*: his highly iconoclastic *Play without a Title* (discussed in chapter 2) and the third play in his "tragic trilogy," *The House of Bernarda Alba*; "A Drama about Women in the Villages of Spain." The stylistic polarity of those two last plays is an indication of the artist's confidence in his own well-developed sense of what will work on stage.

*The House of Bernarda Alba* is Lorca's most realistic play. He prefaced it with this statement: "The poet calls attention to the fact that these three acts are intended as a photographic documentary." His deliberate reference to himself as "the poet" (as opposed to "writer" or "author") signals his continuing commitment to poetry of the theatre. Within those contexts—realism and poetry of the theatre—*The House of Bernarda Alba* is an experiment in economy of means. It obeys the neoclassical unities of time, place, and action. It calls for a tight color range, mostly black costumes against white walls. Lorca is reported to have said of it: "I suppressed many things in this tragedy, many facile songs, many little ballads and verse passages. I want this work to have severity and simplicity."[28]

Just as *Blood Wedding* was inspired by a news clipping, *The House of Bernarda Alba* was also based in actuality. Lorca told Carlos Morla Lynch about a house adjacent to one owned by his family in the village of Valderrubio, where a widow named Frasquita Alba confined and tyrannized her four unmarried daughters. From the patio Lorca was able to overhear conversations and arguments among the women whose existence was poisoned by their isolation from men. According to other sources, the petty jealousies within that tight circle intensified when the eldest daughter—who was ugly, but who had inherited money from her father, who had been her mother's first husband—won a proposal of marriage from a certain Pepe de la Romilla, who was at the same time secretly visiting the youngest daughter.

In making a drama of these materials borrowed from life, Lorca even intended to keep the original names, but his mother cautioned him against provoking a scandal. Frasquita Alba became Bernarda Alba (he refused to give up the real surname, whose literal meaning, "white," was so evocative of virginity, sterility, and emptiness) and Pepe de la Romilla became Pepe el Romano.[29] Lorca added a fifth daughter to the household and gave them all names with strong connotative values: Angustias (anguish), Magdalena (after the weepy biblical Mary Magdalene), Amelia (industrious), Martirio (martyr), and the youngest, Adela, who seems to make an indirect reference to her own name in one of her last speeches: "I have been strong enough to move forward (*adelantarme*)." The rebellious Adela, in her eagerness to take the initiative and seize the moment before time passes her by, is quite the opposite of the passive Doña Rosita, who tries to maintain a serene dignity by ignoring the passage of time. One other name in the play seems to have particular significance, that of the servant La Poncia. Her name is the feminine form of Poncio or Pontius, and although she attempts to get Bernarda Alba to listen to reason, she, in effect, washes her hands of any responsibility for the state of affairs in the household.

Act 1 is set in "a very white room (*habitación blanquísima*) in the interior of Bernarda's house." Lorca's specification of an interior room, repeated in the two succeeding acts, makes it clear that there are to be no windows in the setting; the feeling is one of insulation ("thick walls" are specified) from the outside world. Vincente Cabrera points out in "Poetic Structure in Lorca's *La Casa de Bernarda Alba*" that the whiteness of

the walls decreases in intensity in the course of the
play; they are described as "white" in Act 2, and as
"white with a slight bluish cast" in Act 3. Cabrera suggests that "this gradual decrease corresponds to the
steady and perceptible weakening of Bernarda's control over Adela."[30]

The play opens with the tolling of church bells for
the funeral mass of Bernarda Alba's second husband. La
Poncia and another Servant take advantage of their mistress's absence by stealing food from the household, but
they refuse to give any scraps to a Beggar Woman who
comes to the door. This is the first of several instances
in the play illustrating how the tyranny, selfishness, and
abusiveness of the mistress breeds pettiness, greed,
and ill will in those who are subject to her domination,
that is, her daughters and her senile mother as well as
the servants. The hypocrisy that flourishes in such an
atmosphere is revealed when the Servant curses the
dead man, who had often "lifted her petticoats behind
the corral door," but she breaks into loud lamentations
for him as soon as the women in mourning black return
from church.

Bernarda's first word in the play is the same as her
last word in Act 3: "Silence!" The stage fills up with
"two hundred women," and Bernarda leads them in a
litany for the dead. After the women leave, Bernarda
tells her daughters what to expect henceforth: "During
the eight years of mourning no air from the street shall
enter this house. It will be as if the doors and windows
were walled up with bricks. That's the way it was done
in my father's house and in my grandfather's house."
The daughters, who range in age from Adela, twenty,
to Angustias, thirty-nine, will spend their days with
needle and thread in hand: "That's what it is to be a
woman." Bernarda lashes out at Angustias for looking at
men through a crack in the courtyard door, but as soon
as her daughters leave the room Bernarda solicits La

Poncia's report on the men's gossip and listens avidly to the secondhand stories of Paca la Roseta, "the only loose woman in the village." Bernarda is proud that none of her daughters has ever attracted the attention of a man, for she considers none of the village men in the same class with her family. She orders La Poncia to put away her husband's clothes in a chest. To La Poncia's suggestion that they be given to the poor, Bernarda replies: "Nothing. Not even a button! Not even the handkerchief that covered his face."

In a scene among the daughters, the only subject they discuss is men. Adela, the youngest, has rebelliously put on a green dress, a life-affirming gesture that sets her in contrast to her sisters, in whom all natural impulses have been subjugated or distorted. She is upset, however, to learn that Angustias is going to marry the handsome twenty-five-year-old Pepe el Romano. As the only daughter by Bernarda's first husband, Angustias is independently wealthy. Her sisters have no illusions about the reason for Pepe's interest in the eldest of them. Suddenly, eighty-year-old Maria Josefa, Bernarda's mother, enters, having escaped from the room where she is kept locked up. Wearing flowers on her head and breast, she declares that she is running away to the seashore to get married. Maria Josefa is seized on Bernarda's orders, to be locked up again.

In Act 2, the daughters sit and sew, again talking about men. Angustias is asked to describe her nocturnal conversations with Pepe el Romano through the iron grillwork of her bedroom window. He has been paying court to her every night until about one-thirty in the morning. La Poncia seems suspicious about something when she says that she heard him leave around four the previous night. Later, alone with Adela, La Poncia accuses her of sitting nearly naked at her window with the light on to attract Pepe to her after he left Angustias. La Poncia is concerned about the decency of the house in

which she spends her old age. Adela impetuously replies: "It's already too late."

The song of the reapers on their way to the fields is
heard from the street. The daughters pause and listen
wistfully to the seductive words sung by vigorous male
voices; it is a moment that expresses more vividly than
could any dialogue the psychological effect of being
shut away from the full experience of life.

Angustias enters in a rage, having just discovered
that the picture of Pepe that was under her pillow has
been stolen. Bernarda orders a search of all the rooms,
and the picture is discovered in Martirio's bed. Bernarda beats Martirio. The incident brings out repressed
hostilities among all the daughters. La Poncia tries to
warn Bernarda that more things than she suspects are
going on in the house, but Bernarda has confidence in
her own watchful discipline. Their attention is diverted
by a crowd of gossipers heard in the street, and La
Poncia is sent to investigate. In a terse whispered confrontation, Martirio tells Adela that she saw Pepe embrace her. Martirio is jealous enough to kill, but Adela
insists: "I will have everything."

The news on the street was that a certain unmarried village girl had a child by an unnamed man.
"To hide her shame she killed the baby and put it under some rocks, but the dogs with more compassion
than most creatures uncovered it and, as if guided by
the hand of God, deposited it on her doorstep. Now
they want to kill the girl." Bernarda impassionedly begins to call for the girl's death: "Let whoever tramples
on decency pay for it! . . . Burning coals in the place
where she sinned!" Putting her hands to her belly,
Adela cries "No! No!" in counterpoint to Bernarda's
"Kill her! Kill her!"

The women are eating their evening meal when
Act 3 opens. The sound of a stallion that is locked up
next to the house and kicking the walls interrupts the

conversation. That disturbance is analogous to the emotional stir that any male presence near the house causes among the women within. Angustias has received her engagement ring from Pepe and has spent a great deal of money on furniture. When Adela goes to the courtyard for a breath of fresh air, the suspicious Martirio and Amelia accompany her. She returns from gazing up at the stars and asks her mother why, upon seeing a shooting star, one recites a popular folk invocation to Saint Barbara. Bernarda merely answers that the ancients knew a lot of things that are now forgotten; she accepts tradition as unquestioningly as she marches blindly into the future. In a fascinating article on "'Santa Barbara' and *La Casa de Bernarda Alba*," Judith M. Bull explains in detail the many hagiographical associations upon which Lorca was drawing in order to enhance the significance of Adela's and Bernarda's final actions and dialogue. She concludes: "In his use of popular aspects of the cult of Saint Barbara, Lorca achieves perfect balance between popular tradition and original creation. The rhyme 'Santa Barbara bendita' contains the essence of the tragedy, which is enriched by the dramatic potential of the imagery."[31]

Bernarda and her daughters go off to bed. In a kind of calm before the storm, La Poncia and the other Servant discuss the seething emotions beneath the surface of the apparently well-disciplined household. La Poncia has decided that there is nothing more she can do to avert the coming storm, and, therefore, she will simply "turn her back to it in order not to see it." Adela enters, wearing her petticoat. Seeing the servants, she says she woke up thirsty and came for a drink of water. When they have all gone, Maria Josefa enters with a lamb in her arms, and sings an improvised lullaby to it. She does not see Adela slip through the room and out the courtyard door, but she intercepts Martirio, who was following Adela, and babbles semicoherently about

her ability to have babies despite her hair as white as
foam on the sea. Martirio pushes Maria Josefa back into
her bedroom and locks her in. Then Martirio runs to
the courtyard door and summons Adela, who enters
with her hair disarranged.

The two youngest sisters now understand each
other completely and will never be reconciled. Neither
of them is bothered by the idea of Pepe's marriage to
Angustias since they know that he does not love her,
but Martirio cannot bear to think of Pepe's attraction to
Adela. Adela says that she is willing to live openly as
the mistress of a married man no matter what the villagers will think of her. When a whistle is heard from
outside, Adela tries to rush out, but Martirio blocks the
way and calls their mother. Martirio directs Bernarda's
attention to the bits of straw clinging to Adela's petticoat. Bernarda lunges at Adela, but Adela stands up to
her mother, snatches her cane, and breaks it in two.
The cane is, of course, a symbol of Bernarda's authority, but Lorca's use of canes in *The Audience* (as props
for the White Horses) makes it clear that he also regarded them as phallic symbols. Adela's action is not
only one of self-assertion against a tyrant, but it also
symbolically ends Bernarda's usurpation of the male
role in the household.

The noise of the confrontation brings the servants
and the other sisters. Adela declares triumphantly: "I'll
no longer take orders from anyone but Pepe. . . . I am
his woman." She starts to go to Pepe, but Angustias
holds her back while Bernarda rushes to get her gun. A
shot is heard. Martirio returns with Bernarda and says
that Pepe has been killed. Adela runs out screaming for
Pepe. Martirio tells the others that Pepe actually got
away on his horse, but she lied in order to hurt Adela.
Bernarda says: "It was not my fault. A woman can't
aim." If the shotgun is seen as another phallic symbol,

Bernarda's poor aim is another sign of the arrested masculinization of her character.

A thud is heard from the next room, but the door is locked. La Poncia breaks it down and goes in. She screams. Adela has hanged herself. Bernarda states categorically that her daughter died a virgin. She is to be dressed as a virgin and given a honorable funeral mass and nothing else will be said of it. "Silence!" she commands as the curtain closes.

Some critics suggest that Bernarda's authority within the house will be permanently impaired by Adela's rebellion, while others, more plausibly, given the play's deliberate circular construction, see that the tragedy is not only the death of Adela but also the fact that her death will change nothing in the household. Apart from its importance as a psychological study of women and, of course, as a theatrical work with tremendous impact, this play fascinates critics by what Roberto Sánchez calls "*la última manera de García Lorca*," that is, his "critical stance, a social concern."[32] Anthony Aratari's interpretation is the most extreme in that regard:

The House of Bernarda Alba is Spain itself, Spain become a matriarchy in which men are distrusted and hated, whose essential manhood is unloved, and who in turn make their bodies into a thing to be sold to women they do not love but who have money and property. . . . This is no doubt a frightening picture: to see a great Catholic country run into the ground; but as prophecy it came true. Spain conceived within her house a civil war which took some one million lives, from which she shakily emerged only with the dubious help of Mussolini and Hitler. Lorca's plays are not propaganda. In their complex images he has exposed the terrible fault that walks on four feet right out of the Garden of Eden: the most fundamental human relationship possible, that of man with woman, had foundered: the gears of life had slipped in the heart of Spain.[33]

Whether or not we go so far as to apply a Marxist or other ideological interpretation to Lorca's late plays, we have at least learned from the "unperformable plays" that there is a far more complex subtext to *The House of Bernarda Alba*, *Yerma*, *Doña Rosita the Spinster*, and *Blood Wedding* than is readily apparent.

In a *New York Times* article on October 19, 1980, Arthur Holmberg wrote of "Spain's rediscovery of its great poet of the stage."[34] There is indeed a Lorca renaissance going on in Spain today, and it is as much to Spain's credit as it is to Lorca's. Lorca was a total artist who took seriously the artist's responsibility to provoke people to think, feel, and try to understand more about the world in which we live. To that end he devoted his amazing talents as poet, painter, musician, folk entertainer, and man of the theatre. History has shown that the greatness of a nation depends to a large extent upon the nourishment of its own creative geniuses. With the renewed recognition of Lorca's artistry, Spain may yet enter its second golden age.

# Notes

## 1. THE ARTIST'S LIFE

1. Federico García Lorca, *Obras completas*, vol. 2 (Madrid: Aguilar, 1980), p. 1058.
2. Ibid., p. 1081.
3. Ibid., p. 1115.
4. Marcelle Auclair, *Enfances et mort de García Lorca* (Paris: Editions du Seuil, 1968), p. 72.
5. Ibid., p. 45.
6. Federico García Lorca, *Obras completas*, vol. 1 (Madrid: Aguilar, 1980), p. 1167.
7. Ibid., p. 1056.
8. Mildred Adams, *García Lorca: Playwright and Poet* (New York: George Braziller, 1977), p. 15.
9. Daniel Devoto, "Lecturas de García Lorca," *Revue de la littérature comparée* 33 (October–December 1959), pp. 518–21.
10. José Mora Guarnido, *Federico García Lorca y su mundo: testimonio para una biografía* (Buenos Aires: Losada, 1958), pp. 106–8.
11. Ian Gibson, "Federico García Lorca en Burgos: más artículos olvidados," *Bulletin Hispanique* 69 (January 1967), pp. 179–82.
12. Auclair, pp. 64–65.
13. García Lorca, vol. 1, p. 852.
14. Ibid., p. 1167.
15. Auclair, pp. 75–77.
16. Salvador Dalí, *The Secret Life of Salvador Dalí*, trans. Haakon M. Chevalier (New York: Dial Press, 1942), p. 176.

17. García Lorca, vol. 2, p. 1346.
18. Dalí, p. 84.
19. García Lorca, vol. 1, p. 778.
20. Auclair, p. 155.
21. Ibid., p. 83.
22. Ildefonso-Manuel Gil, ed., *Federico García Lorca* (Madrid: Taurus, 1973), p. 464.
23. García Lorca, vol. 2, p. 6.
24. Gil, p. 464.
25. José Luis Cano, *García Lorca* (Barcelona: Destino, 1974), p. 42.
26. García Lorca, vol. 2, p. 1027.
27. Edward F. Stanton, *The Tragic Myth: Lorca and Cante Jondo* (Lexington: University Press of Kentucky, 1979), pp. 4–6.
28. Auclair, pp. 124–25.
29. Ibid., p. 132.
30. García Lorca, vol. 2, p. 1259.
31. Ibid., p. 1265.
32. Edwin Honig, *García Lorca* (Norfolk, CT: New Directions, 1944), p. 58.
33. Antonina Rodrigo, *García Lorca en Cataluña* (Barcelona: Planeta, 1975), p. 114.
34. Cano, p. 64.
35. Auclair, p. 14.
36. García Lorca, vol. 2, p. 1339.
37. Gil, p. 426.
38. Rodrigo, p. 252.
39. García Lorca, vol. 2, p. 1277.
40. Ibid., p. 1360.
41. Auclair, p. 104.
42. Ibid., p. 101.
43. García Lorca, vol. 2, pp. 1137–38.
44. Ibid., pp. 1356–57.
45. Ibid., p. 1359.
46. José Luis Vila-San-Juan, *García Lorca, Asesinado: toda la verdad* (Barcelona: Planeta, 1975), pp. 50–54.
47. García Lorca, vol. 2, p. 1344.
48. Ibid., p. 1371.

49. Daniel Eisenberg, "A Chronology of Lorca's Visit to New York and Cuba," *Kentucky Romance Quarterly* 24 (1977), pp. 233–50.

50. Herschel Brickell, "A Spanish Poet in New York," *Virginia Quarterly* 21 (1945), p. 391.

51. Auclair, p. 222.

52. Brickell, p. 394.

53. Adams, p. 137.

54. Auclair, p. 230.

55. Rafael Martínez Nadal, *Federico García Lorca and "The Public"* (New York: Schocken Books, 1974), p. 19.

56. Luis Sáenz de la Calzada, *La Barraca: Teatro universitario* (Madrid: Revista de occidente, 1976), p. 169.

57. Auclair, p. 268.

58. Suzanne Byrd, *García Lorca: La Barraca and the Spanish National Theater* (New York: Abra-las–Américas, 1975), p. 45.

59. García Lorca, vol. 2, p. 1067.

60. Ibid., p. 1050.

61. Joaquín Estafanía Moreira, "La Barraca, un intento renovador del teatro popular," *Informaciones* (Madrid, February 13, 1975), p. 8.

62. Luis Sáenz de la Calzada, "La Barraca: teatro universitario," *Revista de occidente* 3 (January 1977), p. 14.

63. García Lorca, vol. 1, p. 1215.

64. Robert Lima, *The Theatre of García Lorca* (New York: Las Americas, 1963), p. 35.

65. Byrd, p. 68.

66. García Lorca, vol. 1, pp. 1216–17).

67. Auclair, pp. 28–29.

68. Ian Gibson, *Granada en 1936 y el asesinato de Federico García Lorca* (Barcelona: Crítica, 1979), p. 43.

69. Vilas San-Juan, p. 232.

70. Ian Gibson, *The Death of Lorca* (Chicago: J. Philip O'Hara, Inc., 1973), p. 41.

71. García Lorca, vol. 2, p. 1126.

72. Ibid.

73. García Lorca, vol. 1, p. 581.

74. Rodrigo, p. 154.

## 2. THE KEY "UNPERFORMABLE PLAYS"

1. Federico García Lorca, *Obras completas,* vol. 2 (Madrid: Aguilar, 1980), p. 975.
2. Ibid., p. 1120.
3. Miguel García Posada, *García Lorca* (Madrid: Escritores de todos los tiempos, 1979), pp. 137–38.
4. Ibid., p. 133.
5. Rafael Martínez Nadal, *Federico García Lorca and "The Public"* (New York: Schocken Books, 1974), p. 30.
6. García Lorca, vol. 2, p. 468.
7. Ibid., pp. 475–76.
8. Martínez Nadal, p. 38.
9. Marie Laffranque, "Poète et Public," *Europe* (August–September 1980), p. 123.
10. García Lorca, vol. 2, p. 482.
11. Ibid., p. 486.
12. Ibid., pp. 500–501.
13. García Lorca, vol. 1, p. 1105.
14. Ibid., p. 447.
15. Martínez Nadal, p. 17.
16. Ibid., p. 20.
17. García Lorca, vol. 2, p. 511.
18. John Brotherton, *The "Pastor-Bobo" in the Spanish Theatre before the Time of Lope de Vega* (London: Tamesis, 1975).
19. García Lorca, vol. 2, p. 526.
20. Ibid., p. 532.
21. Ibid., p. 533.
22. Federico García Lorca, *El Público y Comedia sin título,* ed. with introductions by Rafael Martínez Nadal and Marie Laffranque (Barcelona: Editorial Seix Barral, 1978), p. 53.
23. Martínez Nadal, p. 93.
24. At times, in telling others about this play in progress, Lorca referred to this character as The Poet. In the extant draft, the character is called, in Spanish, *El Autor,* an archaic term for "Manager" or "Director" as well as the more usual "Author." I have used Author as a kind of compromise translation, which seems justified when

considered in the sense of the modern film critic's *auteur*. The archaic usage does force comparison of this character with the Director in *The Audience*.

25. García Lorca, vol. 2, p. 945.
26. Ibid., p. 952.
27. García Lorca, *El Público y Comedia sin título*, pp. 288–89.
28. Ibid., p. 286.
29. Ibid., pp. 299–301.
30. García Lorca, vol. 2, p. 391.
31. Ibid., p. 425.
32. Rupert C. Allen, *The Symbolic World of Federico García Lorca* (Albuquerque: University of New Mexico Press, 1972), pp. 61–157.
33. Farris Anderson, "The Theatrical Design of Lorca's *Así que pasen cinco años*," *Journal of Spanish Studies: Twentieth Century* 7 (Winter 1979), pp. 249–78.
34. Dennis A. Klein, "*Así que pasen cinco anos*: A Search for Sexual Identity," *Journal of Spanish Studies: Twentieth Century* 3 (1975), pp. 115–23.
35. R. G. Knight, "Federico García Lorca's *Así que pasen cinco años*," *Bulletin of Hispanic Studies* 43 (1966), pp. 32–46.
36. Auclair, pp. 236–37.

### 3.   MUSIC AND THE MUSICALITY OF THE EARLY POETRY

1. Federico García Lorca, *Obras completas*, vol. 2 (Madrid: Aguilar, 1980), p. 1138.
2. Ian Gibson, "Federico García Lorca, su maestro de música y un artículo olvidado," *Insula* (March 1966), p. 14.
3. Ibid.
4. Ubaldo Bardi, "Federico García Lorca, Musician; Equipment for a Bibliography," *García Lorca Review* 9 (Spring 1981), pp. 30–42.
5. Marcelle Auclair, *Enfances et mort de García Lorca* (Paris: Seuil, 1968), p. 59.

6.  Federico García Lorca, *Obras completas* (Madrid: Aguilar, 1967), p. 1801.
7.  Ibid., p. 1698.
8.  Auclair, p. 59.
9.  Edward F. Stanton, *The Tragic Myth: Lorca and Cante Jondo* (Lexington: University Press of Kentucky, 1979), p. ix.
10. Marcelle Schveitzer, "Souvenirs" in *Federico García Lorca*, ed. Louis Parrot (Paris: Seghers, 1949), p. 193.
11. Auclair, p. 59.
12. Gibson, p. 14.
13. García Lorca, 1967 ed., p. 1744.
14. Federico García Lorca, *Obras completas*, vol. 1 (Madrid: Aguilar, 1980), pp. 1074–75.
15. Gibson, p. 14.
16. García Lorca, vol. 1, p. 5.
17. García Lorca, vol. 1, p. 51.
18. Ibid., p. 52.
19. Ibid., pp. 30–31.
20. Ibid., p. 127.
21. Ibid., p. 97.
22. Ibid., p. 98.
23. Auclair, p. 88.
24. García Lorca, vol. 1, p. 1006.
25. Ibid., p. 1013.
26. Ibid., p. 1015.
27. Ibid., p. 162.
28. Ibid., p. 153.
29. Ibid., p. 157.
30. Ibid., p. 158.
31. Ibid., p. 208.
32. Ibid., p. 285.
33. Ibid., p. 265.
34. Ibid., p. 267.
35. Ibid., p. 285.
36. Ibid., p. 297.
37. Carlos Feal Deibe, *Eros y Lorca* (Barcelona: Edhasa, 1973), pp. 32–36.
38. García Lorca, vol. 1, p. 38.
39. Ibid., p. 313.

40. Ibid., p. 333.
41. Ibid., p. 389.
42. Manuel Durán, "Así que pasen cincuenta años: *El Romancero gitano* visto desde 1978," *García Lorca Review* 7 (Spring 1979), p. 19.
43. J. B. Trend, *Lorca and the Spanish Poetic Tradition* (Oxford: Basil Blackwell, 1956), p. 5.
44. García Lorca, 1967, p. 1796.
45. Federico García Lorca, *The Gypsy Ballads of Federico García Lorca,* trans. with Introduction by Rolfe Humphries (Bloomington: Indiana University Press, 1969), p. 17.
46. García Lorca, 1967, p. 1795.
47. García Lorca, vol. 2, p. 1259.
48. Auclair, p. 163.
49. García Lorca, vol. 1, p. 426.
50. Ibid., p. 429.
51. Ibid., p. 409.
52. Ibid., p. 420.
53. Ibid., p. 398.
54. Roy Campbell, *Lorca; An Appreciation of his Poetry* (New Haven: Yale University Press, 1952), p. 44.
55. García Lorca, vol. 1, p. 399.
56. Ibid., p. 402.
57. Gibson, p. 14.

4. THE VISUAL ARTS

1. Patrick Fourneret, "Los Dibujos humanísimos de Federico Garía Lorca," *Trece de nieve* (December 1976), p. 150.
2. Ibid., p. 163.
3. Federico García Lorca, *Obras completas,* vol. 1 (Madrid: Aguilar, 1980), pp. 1071–72.
4. Federico García Lorca, *Obras completas,* vol. 2 (Madrid: Aguilar, 1980), p. 1348.
5. Ibid., p. 1347.
6. David K. Loughran, *Federico García Lorca: The Poetry of Limits* (London: Tamesis Books, Ltd., 1978), p. 204.

7. Gregorio Prieto, *Dibujos de Federico García Lorca* (Madrid: Afrodisio Aguado, 1949), p. 7.

8. Gregorio Prieto Muñoz, *García Lorca as a Painter*, trans. J. McLachlan and J. D. Beazley (London: The De La More Press, 1967), p. 8.

9. Guillermo Díaz Plaja, *Federico García Lorca* (Buenos Aires: Kraft, 1948), p. 127.

10. Federico García Lorca, *Cartas, postales, poemas y dibujos*, ed. Antonio Gallego Morell (Madrid: Moneda y Crédito, 1968), p. 55.

11. "Drawing; Sketches of the Banned," *Time* (August 20, 1965), p. 50.

12. Fernando Arrabal, personal interview (April 23, 1982, Cedar Falls, Iowa).

13. "Drawing," *Time*, p. 50.

14. Díaz Plaja, p. 281.

15. García Lorca, vol. 1, p. 1065.

16. C. B. Morris, *Surrealism and Spain, 1920–1936* (Cambridge: University Press, 1972), p. 49.

17. García Lorca, vol. 2, p. 1300.

18. Ibid., p. 234.

19. Rupert Allen, "A Commentary on Lorca's *El Paseo de Buster Keaton*," *Hispanófila* 48 (May 1973), p. 24.

20. Ibid., pp. 25, 32.

21. Barbara N. Davis, "Lorca, Surrealism, and the *Teatro Breve*," *García Lorca Review* 6 (Fall 1978), p. 99.

22. Virginia Higginbotham, "Lorca's Apprenticeship in Surrealism," *Romanic Review* 61 (1970), p. 113.

23. Robert C. Havard, "Lorca's Buster Keaton," *Bulletin of Hispanic Studies* 54 (January 1977), p. 13.

24. Allen, p. 34.

25. Higginbotham, p. 113.

26. Davis, p. 104.

27. Richard Diers, "Introductory Note to *Trip to the Moon*," *New Directions in Prose and Poetry* 18 (New York: New Directions, 1964), pp. 33–34.

28. Federico García Lorca, *Trip to the Moon*, trans. Bernice G. Duncan, in *New Directions in Prose and Poetry* 18 (New York: New Directions, 1964), pp. 35–41.

29. Virginia Higginbotham, "El Viaje de García Lorca a la luna," *Insula* 23 (January 1968), p. 1.
30. J. F. Aranda, "Surrealismo español en el cine," *Insula* 29 (December 1974), p. 19.
31. García Lorca, *Trip to the Moon*, p. 41.
32. Aranda, p. 19; Morris, p. 127.
33. Diers, p. 35.

## 5. FOLK ENTERTAINMENTS

1. Federico de Onís, "García Lorca, folklorista," *Revista Hispanica Moderna* 6 (July–October 1940), p. 370.
2. Virginia Higginbotham, *The Comic Spirit of Federico García Lorca* (Austin: University of Texas Press, 1975), p. 30.
3. Federico García Lorca, *El Público y Comedia sin título,* ed. with introductions by R. Martínez Nadal and Marie Laffranque (Barcelona: Seix Barral, 1978), p. 294.
4. Federico García Lorca, *Obras completas,* vol. 1 (Madrid: Aguilar, 1980), p. 1215.
5. Ibid., p. 1169.
6. Federico García Lorca, *Obras completas,* vol. 2 (Madrid: Aguilar, 1980), pp. 61–62.
7. García Lorca, vol. 1, p. 1212.
8. García Lorca, vol. 2, p. 539.
9. Ibid., p. 555.
10. Ibid., p. 551.
11. Ibid., p. 329.
12. Ibid., p. 553.
13. Higginbotham, p. 38.
14. Francisco García Lorca, "Introduction," *Five Plays by Lorca* (New York: New Directions, 1963), p. 8.
15. García Lorca, vol. 1, p. 1172.
16. Ibid., p. 1174.
17. Daniel Devoto, "Notas sobre el elemento tradicionalista en la obra de García Lorca," *Filología* 2 (1950), p. 326.
18. García Lorca, vol. 1, p. 1173.
19. García Lorca, vol. 2, p. 256.

20. Robert Lima, *The Theatre of García Lorca* (New York: Las Americas, 1963), p. 123.
21. García Lorca, vol. 1, p. 1173.
22. García Lorca, vol. 2, p. 269.
23. Ibid., p. 277.
24. Ibid., p. 320.
25. Ibid., p. 992.
26. Suzanne Byrd, *García Lorca: La Barraca and the Spanish National Theater* (New York: Abra-las-Américas, 1975), p. 33.
27. Ibid., p. 18.
28. Estelle Trépanier, "García Lorca et La Barraca," *Revue d'Histoire du Théâtre* (1966), p. 168.
29. Luis Sáenz de la Calzada, "La Barraca, teatro universitario," *Revista de occidente* 3 (January 1977), p. 14.
30. García Lorca, vol. 2, pp. 1051–52.
31. Pablo Suero, *Figuras contemporáneas* (Buenos Aires: Americana, 1943), p. 299.
32. Sáenz de la Calzada, p. 8.
33. García Lorca, vol. 2, p. 1070.
34. Trépanier, p. 169.
35. Byrd, p. 39.
36. García Lorca, vol. 2, 1053.
37. Byrd, p. 82.
38. Ibid., p. 38.

## 6.   NEW DIRECTIONS IN POETRY

1. José Ortega, "*Poeta en Nueva York*, Alienación Social y libertad poética," *Cuadernos Hispanoamericanos* (February 1980), pp. 350–52.
2. Derek Harris, *García Lorca: Poeta en Nueva York* (London: Grant and Cutter, Ltd., 1978), p. 15.
3. Ibid., p. 9.
4. Betty Jean Craige, *Lorca's 'Poet in New York;' The Fall into Consciousness* (Lexington: The University Press of Kentucky, 1977), pp. 8–9, 84–86.
5. Richard L. Predmore, *Lorca's New York Poetry* (Durham: Duke University Press, 1980), p. 34.

6. Federico García Lorca, *Obras completas,* vol. 2 (Madrid: Aguilar, 1980), p. 1365.

7. Angel del Río, "Introduction," *Poet in New York by Federico García Lorca,* trans. Ben Belitt (New York: Grove Press, 1955), p. xvii.

8. Harris, p. 28.

9. Federico García Lorca, *Obras completas,* vol. 1 (Madrid: Aguilar, 1980), p. 1127.

10. Ibid., p. 459.

11. Ibid., p. 1127.

12. Ibid., p. 1130.

13. Ibid., p. 490.

14. Ibid., p. 496.

15. Harris, p. 57.

16. D. R. Harris, "The Religious Theme in Lorca's *Poeta en Nueva York," Bulletin of Hispanic Studies* (October 1977), pp. 322–24.

17. Angel del Río, pp. xxxi–xxxii.

18. García Lorca, vol. 1, p. 529.

19. Ibid., p. 536.

20. Ibid., p. 538.

21. Ibid., p. 542.

22. Edwin Honig, *García Lorca* (Norfolk, CT: New Directions, 1944), p. 104.

23. Marcelle Auclair, *Enfances et mort de García Lorca* (Paris: Seuil, 1968), p. 23.

24. Auclair, p. 19.

25. Edward F. Stanton, *The Tragic Myth: Lorca and Cante Jondo* (Lexington: University Press of Kentucky, 1979), p. 50.

26. Auclair, pp. 19–22.

27. Ibid., pp. 26–28.

28. Ibid., pp. 22–23.

29. Ibid., p. 28.

30. Ibid., pp. 24–25.

31. Ibid., p. 25.

32. William Carlos Williams, "Federico García Lorca" in *Lorca: A Collection of Critical Essays,* ed. Manuel Duran (Englewood Cliffs, NJ: Prentice-Hall, Inc., 1962), p. 24.

33. García Lorca, vol. 1, p. 555.
34. Ibid., p. 557.
35. Ibid., p. 558.
36. Auclair, p. 30.
37. Miguel García Posada, *García Lorca* (Madrid: Escritores de todos los tiempos, 1979), pp. 108–9.
38. Federico García Lorca, *The Selected Poems,* ed. Francisco García Lorca and Donald M. Allen (New York: New Directions, 1955), pp. 155, 157.
39. Honig, p. 93.
40. García Posada, p. 109.
41. García Lorca, vol. 1, p. 573.
42. Ibid.
43. Ibid., p. 583.
44. Ibid., p. 581.
45. Ibid., p. 589.

## 7.  THEATRE AS SYNTHESIS

1. Roberto G. Sánchez, "Lorca, the Post-War Theatre and the Conflict of Generations," *Kentucky Romance Quarterly* 19 (1972), pp. 17–29.
2. Frank P. Casa, "Theater after Franco: The First Reaction," *Hispanofila* 6 (May 1979), pp. 109–22.
3. Federico García Lorca, *Obras completas,* vol. 2 (Madrid: Aguilar, 1980), p. 1088.
4. Marie Laffranque, *Les Idées aeshéthiques de Federico García Lorca* (Paris: Centre de Recherches Hispaniques, 1967), p. 21.
5. Federico García Lorca, *Obras completas,* vol. 1 (Madrid: Aguilar, 1980), pp. 1215–16.
6. García Lorca, vol. 2, pp. 1086–87.
7. Ibid., p. 1119.
8. Ibid., p. 1124.
9. One example: Manuel Blanco-González, "Lorca: The Tragic Trilogy," *Drama Critique* 9 (Spring 1966), pp. 91–97.
10. Francesca Colecchia, "The Religious Ambience in the Trilogy; A Definition," *García Lorca Review* 10 (Spring 1982), pp. 32, 41.

11. Harriet S. Turner, "Circularity and Closure in Lorca's Trilogy" in *The World of Nature in the Works of Federico García Lorca,* ed. Joseph W. Zdenek, Winthrop College Studies on Major Modern Writers (Rock Hill, South Carolina, 1980), pp. 101–15.

12. García Lorca, vol. 2, p. 652.

13. Ibid., p. 657.

14. Federico García Lorca, *Three Tragedies,* trans. James Graham-Luján and Richard L. O'Connell (New York: New Directions, 1955), p. 98.

15. García Lorca, vol. 2, p. 662.

16. Robert Lima, *The Theatre of García Lorca* (New York: Las Americas, 1963), p. 188.

17. Grace Alvarez-Altman, "Ten Years of *The García Lorca Review;* Highlights and its Future," *García Lorca Review* 10 (Spring 1982), pp. 43–44.

18. Dennis A. Klein, "Christological Imagery in Lorca's *Yerma,*" *García Lorca Review* 6 (Spring 1978), pp. 35–42.

19. Robert Skloot, "Theme and Image in Lorca's *Yerma,*" *Drama Survey* 5 (Summer 1966), pp. 151–61.

20. García Lorca, vol. 2, pp. 727–28.

21. Ibid., pp. 1069, 1070.

22. Ibid., p. 1078.

23. Ibid., p. 1069.

24. Ibid., p. 1078.

25. Ibid., pp. 1113–14.

26. Ibid., pp. 752–53.

27. Kathleen Dolan, "Time, Irony, and Negation in Lorca's Last Three Plays," *Hispanica* 63 (September 1980), p. 517.

28. Sánchez, pp. 25–26.

29. Marcelle Auclair, *Enfances et mort de García Lorca* (Paris: Seuil, 1968), pp. 334–37.

30. Vicente Cabrera, "Poetic Structure in Lorca's *La Casa de Bernarda Alba,*" *Hispania* 61 (September 1978), p. 466.

31. Judith M. Bull, "'Santa Barbara' and *La Casa de Bernarda Alba,*" *Bulletin of Hispanic Studies* 47 (April 1970), p. 123.

32. Roberto G. Sánchez, "La Ultima manera de Federico

García Lorca," *Papeles de Son Armadans* 50 (January 1970), p. 101.

33. Anthony Aratari, "The Tragedies of García Lorca," *Commonweal* 62 (August 12, 1955), p. 475.

34. Arthur Holmberg, "Five Years after Franco, Lorca is Alive Again in Spain," *New York Times* (October 19, 1980), Sec. 2, p. 3.

# Bibliography

## WORKS BY FEDERICO GARCÍA LORCA

*Obras completas*. Madrid: Aguilar, 1967.

*Cartas, postales, poemas, y dibujos*. Ed. Antonio Gallego Morell. Madrid: Editorial Monoda y Crédito, 1968.

*El Público y Comedia sin título; Dos obras teatrales póstumas*. Eds. Rafael Martínez Nadal and Marie Laffranque. Barcelona: Seix Barral, 1978.

*Obras completas*. 2 vols. Madrid: Aguilar, 1980.


## WORKS BY FEDERICO GARCÍA LORCA IN ENGLISH TRANSLATION

*Three Tragedies*. Trans. James Graham-Luján and Richard L. O'Connell. New York: New Directions, 1947.

*Poet in New York*. Trans. Ben Belitt. New York: Grove Press, Inc., 1955.

*The Selected Poems of Federico Garía Lorca*. Eds. Francisco García Lorca and Donald M. Allen. New York: New Directions, 1955.

*Five Plays by Lorca; Comedies and Tragicomedies*. Trans. James Graham-Luján and Richard L. O'Connell. New York: New Directions, 1963.

*Trip to the Moon*. Trans. Bernice G. Duncan. *New Directions in Prose and Poetry* 18. New York: New Directions, 1964.

*The Gypsy Ballads of Federico García Lorca*. Trans. Rolfe

Humphries. Bloomington: Indiana University Press, 1969.

*Divan and Other Writings*. Trans. Edwin Honig. Providence: Copper Beech Press, 1977.

*The Cricket Sings; Poems and Songs for Children*. Trans. Will Kirkland. New York: New Directions, 1980.

*Deep Song and Other Prose*. Ed. and trans. Christopher Maurer. New York: New Directions, 1980.

## BIBLIOGRAPHIES

*García Lorca; A Selectively Annotated Bibliography of Criticism*. Ed. Francesca Colecchia. New York: Garland Publishing Co., Inc., 1979.

*The World of Federico García Lorca: A General Bibliographic Survey*. Eds. Joseph L. Laurenti and Joseph Siracusa. Metuchen, NJ: Scarecrow Press, 1974.

## BOOKS IN ENGLISH ABOUT LORCA

Adams, Mildred. *García Lorca: Playwright and Poet*. New York: George Braziller, 1977.

Allen, Rupert C. *The Symbolic World of Federico García Lorca*. Albuquerque: University of New Mexico Press, 1972.

———. *Psyche and Symbol in the Theatre of Federico García Lorca*. Austin: University of Texas Press, 1974.

Craige, Betty Jean. *Lorca's "Poet in New York"; The Fall into Consciousness*. Lexington: University Press of Kentucky, 1977.

Duran, Manuel, ed. *Lorca; A Collection of Critical Essays*. Englewood Cliffs, NJ: Prentice-Hall, Inc., 1962.

Higginbotham, Virginia. *The Comic Spirit of Federico García Lorca*. Austin: University of Texas Press, 1975.

Lima, Robert. *The Theatre of García Lorca*. New York: Las Americas, 1963.

Loughran, David K. *Federico García Lorca; The Poetry of Limits*. London: Tamesis Books, 1978.

Martínez Nadal, Rafael. *Federico García Lorca and "The Public."* New York: Schocken Books, 1974.

Stanton, Edward F. *The Tragic Myth; Lorca and Cante Jondo.* Lexington: University Press of Kentucky, 1979.

## BOOKS IN SPANISH OR FRENCH ABOUT LORCA

Auclair, Marcelle. *Enfances et mort de García Lorca.* Paris: Editions du Seuil, 1968.

Cano, José Luis. *García Lorca; Biografía ilustrada.* Barcelona: Ediciones Destino, 1969.

Díaz Plaja, Guillermo. *Federico García Lorca.* Buenos Aires: Kraft, 1948.

Eisenberg, Daniel. *"Poeta en Nueva York"; Historia y problemas de un texto de Lorca.* Barcelona: Ariel, 1976.

Feal Deibe, Carlos. *Eros y Lorca.* Barcelona: Edhasa, 1973.

García Posada, Miguel. *García Lorca.* Madrid: Escritores de todos los tiempos, 1979.

Gibson, Ian. *Granada en 1936 y el asesinato de Federico García Lorca.* Barcelona: Editorial Crítica, 1979.

Gil, Ildefonso-Manuel, ed. *Federico García Lorca.* Madrid: Taurus, 1973.

Laffranque, Marie. *Federico García Lorca.* Paris: Seghers, 1966.

———. *Les Idées esthétiques de Federico García Lorca.* Paris: Centre de Recherches Hispaniques, 1967.

Morla Lynch, Carlos. *En España con Federico García Lorca.* Madrid: Aguilar, 1958.

Rodrigo, Antonina. *García Lorca en Cataluña.* Barcelona: Planeta, 1975.

Sánchez, Roberto G. *García Lorca; Estudio sobre su teatro.* Madrid: Jura, 1950.

Vila-San-Juan, José Luis. *García Lorca, Asesinado: toda la verdad.* Barcelona: Planeta, 1975.

# Index